rappers rappin'

Cover Photograph: Phil Parker. Redferns
Photographs: Redferns, Pictorial Press Ltd
Printed by: Staples of Rochester, Kent.
Copyright: Music Maker Publications plc.
Designed by: David Houghton
Published by: Castle Communications plc, A29 Barwell Business Park,
Leatherhead Road, Chessington, Surrey KT9 2NY.

ISBN: 1 86074 1339

rappers rappin'

★ the story of the freshest sound
around from rap's 'maddest' and 'baddest'

compiled and edited by dan goldstein

contents

★ introduction

A voice in the wilderness. Black people's CNN. A view from the underground. Rap music is all this and so much more. What started as a novel musical style among the black and Hispanic neighbourhoods of New York City has – in less than two decades – revolutionised popular culture on a global scale. To say its effects have been far reaching would be a gross understatement. It's changed the way a nation of people eat, sleep, think and live in the modern world.

Rap's roots can be traced back to the block parties and playgrounds of the Bronx and upper Manhattan. Here early innovators such as Kool Herc, Grandmaster Flash and Afrika Bambaataa pioneered the use of two decks and a mixer to keep the bustling dance crowds content. It wasn't long before words were added and rap, as we know it, was born.

However, at this time the music's popularity was strictly street level – existing solely on tapes of live shows distributed among friends. That all changed in 1980. 'Rapper Delight' by the Sugarhill gang was to rap what 'Rock Around The Clock' was to rock 'n' roll. A huge commercial hit, the rap community has barely paused for breath since.

Initially much of the music was flamboyant and fanciful – music to party to rather than express

anger – but as it matured, so did the complexity
of the sentiments expressed. 'The Message' by
Grandmaster Flash & The Furious Five was rap's
first rallying call – a baton subsequently picked
up by the actively pro-black Public Enemy. They,
more than anyone, politicised the genre and
alongside everyone from NWA to Ice-T, epitomised
rap's ability to open the lines of communication
for a disenfranchised and largely powerless
minority.

Still certain critics missed the point, jumping on
rappers from a great height for telling it how it
is rather than how they would like it to be. But
to say all hip-hop is violent, profane or even
politically incorrect is nonsense. Like a great
oak, rap has sprouted many branches – the party
pop of MC Hammer and Jazzy Jeff & The Fresh
Prince; the surreal art rap of De La Soul and A
Tribe Called Quest; the west coast nihilism of
G-Funk practitioners Dr Dre and Snoop; and
lately, the mind-over-matter musings of the
multi-talented, nine-strong Wu-Tang Clan.

Indeed, the reason rap remains the most
consistently essential and innovative of all
modern musics is its ability to adapt to the times
and constantly reinvent itself. An ever changing
force, 'Rappers Rappin'' is one chapter in an
ongoing story.

Andy Cowan
Editor
Hip-Hop Connection

1

coolio

A Compton-born rapper who has taken longer than most to make an impact on the public consciousness, Coolio can trace his roots right back to seminal West Coast collective the World Class Wreckin' Cru. After leaving the Cru he recorded a succession of singles and albums which, for one reason or another, were never rleased. An extended, cocaine-laden interlude then interrupted his recording career, followed by a period of re-hab during which Coolio worked as a fire-fighter. On returning to recording he signed to Tommy Boy Records, and within a year had penned 'Gangsta's Paradise', the single which shattered all records by becoming the first rap track to enter the UK charts at No.1

★ coolio

"I've been around for a while," he says with conviction. "I ain't new to this. I was one of the first LA rappers to start making records. I was doing the talent shows with other rappers and we were all getting 'put on' to do small labels.

"Coming from Compton, I knew Dr Dre and Ice-T – I even toured with him and Ice Cube. I did tours with Dre when he was with the World Class Wreckin' Cru. We were cool, I never had a beef with Dre. I even signed to Ruthless Records for a while, but things kinda didn't work out there. No-one got around to me, so I quit. There was no anger towards them, but I just had to move on."

Coolio started using cocaine, which he was hooked onto while smoking joints. Before he knew what hit him, he was free-basing his career into oblivion. "Everyone was doing it," he recalls. "And no-one knew of the side effects of the drug. The drug ain't safe. I had to really force myself to quit, I couldn't take it any more.

"When Tommy Boy first heard my stuff, they wanted to sign me on with a single deal," he remembers, "but I kept bombarding them with material and I went for a single deal, then an EP deal and eventually through to an album contract. I persisted because I believe in what I'm doing."

"'County Line' [Coolio's first single on Tommy Boy in 1994] is about my experiences on the Welfare. The song is based on fact. Looking at it, it seems a little crazy, but it all happened to me. I'm just dropping reality in the only way I know how. Real message and phat beats.

"My rhymes are based on reality. But I always try to find something positive to say. I'm talking about a place where everything is cool...

"I started fighting fires because I had a drug problem. I needed to get away. It was like a boot camp. I was running every day and slowly I started to feel good again."

On the record industry...

"Have a good lawyer," he counsels. "And get your contracts read. If you know you are good and have confidence in yourself and you know that the record company wants you, then make things work to your advantage. I feel that it is better to be broke of your own accord than let somebody else put you in the position of being broke.

"A lot of people are just in it for the money. I'm not. I'm in it because I love hip-hop and because I'm tired of seeing brothers getting dicked. I'm going to teach them to do the business right – then they can teach somebody else and pretty soon nobody will be stupid anymore.

On his background...

"Growing up wasn't that hard. Until I was about 11, things were alright for me. And then you start getting into the manhood stage, when you start developing the traits that are really going to carry you through life. It became difficult around that time 'cos I had no dad in the home, no brothers, so basically the streets had to teach me how to be a man... A woman can't really teach you that. That's why a lot of young black men don't really have it altogether upstairs, because they had no real serious male influence on the attitudes that they have because they don't really have a [positive] catalyst in their life. Unless they have a really strong mother."

Were you one of those misguided youths doing crazy shit?

"Well, not so much. I wasn't that bad a kid. I got into a few things. Mostly I did shit that I didn't get caught for."

Bangin'?

"Man, we were just experimenting. Back then, bangin' wasn't no big thing. Really, it was just cliquing up – whoever lived in your neighbourhood, you were down with, and of course, we had names.

When I was bangin' we were just fist-fighting. Occasionally someone would get stabbed, or get hit with a stick or a bottle. Nothing too serious. You get out there and scrap, and if you get your ass whooped, you take your ass home. We weren't killing each other back then. Then crack came... And everything changed. Everyone started having guns, everyone wanted money, kids wouldn't play anymore 'cos they were selling dope. Basically, everyone wanted to be a baller [dope dealer]. Those who weren't sellers were smokers. And, unfortunately, I fell into that smoker category – but everyone's already heard about all that."

That's when you went up to San Jose to live with your dad, and spent a sting as a fire-fighter?

"Yeah, and I started getting back into hip-hop."

So when did you start rapping?

"15. That's was in 19...somethin'," Coolio catches himself and laughs. "Naw, who cares? I started rapping around 1979. I'm 32 years old. I think my strong points are my ability to adapt and change. When hip-hop makes a change, I change. In the early days, lyrics were important but – shit – nobody was really dope. Everyone was pretty much talking about themselves, all their rhymes were pretty much braggadocios until 'The Message' by Grandmaster Flash & The Furious Five came along. And then people started talking about things. That was the turning point for me. I was a big fan of Melle Mel [featured rapper on 'The Message']. I just started doing talent shows, and got involved with [LA hip-hop radio station] K-Day. They had this thing called The Performing Arts Program, run by Rory Kaufman for kids – it was for rappers, singers, dancers. We'd go around to high- schools, did dances. Then we started doing it on our own. Me and my homie Spoon [who he also refers to as his 'brother'] deejayed weddings.

"When my homeboy D-Dog got married, we wrote a rhyme for that – made his wife cry! That was our wedding present to him. After that, we started busting raps for other couples at their weddings for like $50 extra. We just changed the names. I started trying to make money doing it. I was just rapping, loving hip-hop. We'd sit in my '64 Dodge Scamp, and my homeboy Billy Boy would beat on the back beat with a half a vacuum cleaner hose and a screwdriver, making a beat so we could rap over it. Back in the day, we called ourselves NUSKOOL (New Underground Systematically Killin' Old Lyrics). I rapped every day. My life was a big-ass rap tour for no money. We used to freestyle, but it wasn't as complicated as it is today. I had to learn how to freestyle. You don't just have to do it in order to be competitive, 'cos I'll be damned if I go into a club, someone starts ripping my ass and I can't come back. We used to battle for names. We'd say, 'If I win, you can't use your name anymore, you have to change it'."

You ever lose your name?

"Once. I was Boo Daddy. I'm glad I lost that one. Then I became Coolio. Never lost that one – nobody could take that motherfucka! I've come a long way, my skills have increased dramatically. Man, I rapped at a grand opening for a Church's Chicken back in the day. I don't give a fuck. I love to rap, and if it didn't pay, I'd still be rapping, straight up. I rapped free for 13 years."

Before launching his solo career Coolio was lead rapper of WC & The Maad Circle's 'Ain't A Damn Thing Changed' LP. Since then WC has acted as a live 'hype man' for Ice Cube and, in '95, released the critically lauded album, 'Curb Servin''. How did your work with WC influence your style?

"I was a little stuck in my old skool ways in terms of [rap] tone and delivery. Dub [aka WC] helped me step into the '80s. Our live stage shows were on point – true emcees. Me and Dub – we were on time. I knew when he was running out of breath, he knew when I was. We anticipated each other's moves on stage. A lot of the east coast groups have them. The Alkaholiks [a neighbouring LA crew] have 'em. I'm gonna tell you who has the routines – I'm gonna give 'em props up the ass: The Lost Boyz. They're a new group [on Uptown/MCA], but I saw them perform at the last Gavin Convention, and they've got routines. That's what me and Dub were about – routines and skills!

"A lot of people know this about me. I've been a chronic asthmatic all my life. I've got machines, I've been hospitalised for asthma more times than I can count."

Why do you still smoke cigarettes?

"We don't even need to talk about that, it's too depressing. But I want to quit.

That's something I'm fighting now."

There's worse addictions...

"Well, not when you have asthma. I smoke because... shit, I have problems just like everyone else. I told myself when I finished my first solo album 'It Takes A Thief', 'I'mma quit smoking'. Then it was, 'When I go gold, I'll quit smoking'. Then it was, 'If I go platinum, I'll quit smoking'. Now it's just, 'Damn, I wish I could quit smoking'."

How does it feel to have blown up?

"It's worse than when I was broke. I got more problems now. Now I have to give a fuck. People are coming at me way different now. People want me to take care of them, coming at me like I owe 'em."

What about the worldwide touring? Did you see amazing things?

"Man, I've already done everything. If my career was over tomorrow, I wouldn't be mad. I'm not content of course – it doesn't stop – but I've been so blessed, man, y'know, with the amount of attention and respect that I've gotten. As far as seeing amazing things, I... I don't know. Just seeing how different people live. I've been to Japan. I heard some dope emcees there... ripping, in Japanese."

Did you like England?

"I didn't like England that much because of the food. But the people were cool, nobody gave me any problems, I didn't experience any racial prejudice. I went clubbing a bit. It was cool, but they're on that jungle shit. I can't get into that. They'll take a song, speed it up to like 45, and then add a wild-ass damn-near pop-that-coochie beat. It's some bullshit man. I heard some cool shit though, too. Darkman. He's dope."

On his modern-day material...

The hype from 'It Takes A Thief' has died down, but you're still rolling. You have the 'Gangsta's Paradise' single from the soundtrack to Dangerous Minds and another new song on the Clueless soundtrack, 'Rollin' With My Homies'...

"The lyrics on 'Rollin' With My Homies' are the original lyrics to 'Fantastic Voyage' [Coolio's second solo single but first major breakthrough hit]. The lyrics on the album were the rewrite. And 'Gangsta's Paradise', I had to change the lyrics on that so many times to get the sample clearance. Stevie [Wonder, whose 'Pastime Paradise' the single liberally samples from] wasn't clearing nothing with cursing! I even had to change 'Mack 10' to just '10'!"

'Gangsta's Paradise' is a lot more solemn and 'gangsta' in terms of content than anything on 'It Takes A Thief', where even the roughest scenarios were depicted with levity. What's up with the change?

"Well, y'know... I'm Coolio," he says leaning back with a cool, thoughtful smile. "I can do anything. I know about that side of life. It's not the life I chose to live, but if you take a real close listen to that song, it's more of a cry for help than a braggadocio gangsta rap song. I know people who really feel that way, who don't really like the life they're living, but who don't really have any other options." ∎

2

de la soul

Media-styled 'hippy' rappers Posdnous, Trugoy the Dove and Pasemaster Mace were Long Island contemporaries of (among others) A Tribe Called Quest and Queen Latifah. With its lilting rhythms, catchy samples and off-the-wall sense of humour, their first album, 'Three Feet High And Rising', was one of the first rap LPs to 'cross over' into the mainstream when it was released in 1989. Two years later, 'De La Soul is Dead' had a harder edge and, despite getting a mauling from the critics, succeeded in keeping this uncompromising trio in the public eye. 'Buhloone Mindstate' (1993) marked a return to the lighter style of De La Soul's début, while maintaining their reputation as a group which simply refuses to hide from serious issues.

★ de la soul

Pace Master Mace breaks the ice: "Our album ['Three Feet High And Rising'] was an example set for people to be more creative and do what they want to do, don't fit themselves into the category that rap has been in for a long time."

Everyone agreed that hip-hop had arrived at its own series of stereotypes. You either had to have a gun on the cover or a thick gold chain to fit the mould. Not so with the most creative, whacked out and spaced album of 1989. It even arrived replete with illustrated flowers on its fluorescent front cover – a move not witnessed before in rap circles.

"It wasn't meant to be different," says Trugoy the Dove Dave. "Just that there was a difference in the beginning. We never came off like any other B-Boy, having the gold chain or anything like that. We didn't set aside and put in our minds that we got to be different; it just came out that way."

On the album, De La Soul show that both well-known and obscure samples can provide the basis for interesting songs. "Songs come from any direction," reveals Trugoy. "The samples can come first, the music or the concept of the song can come first or the rhymes come first. It can come from any direction."

"In all of our houses we have records from our parents that we take from," explains Posdnous. "You know, even now while I'm here, I'm searching in the record stores. I just came from one. I'm crazy on records. This group is always looking for things. We're always looking for certain things to sample. Ask the Jungles [Brothers]. To bring music up to a higher level... Sampling is not always going to be here. It goes in cycles, from sampling, to live music, back to straight up drums. A good producer and a good artist is going to keep up on top of that; you just can't lean on sampling.

"I don't mean that sampling has come to its end," he clarifies, "but it's not going to be here forever. In the beginning, everyone sampled a basic kick and snare. Now, the thing that everybody is dealing with is loops. There are still a lot of nice things to take from it. As long as on the legal side the original artists don't have any beef, it will be around for a long time."

"It's true, the musician and artist makes use of what he or she has," Posdnous agrees. "Then it was all about two turntables, that's all it was about. Now sampling is taking your favourite loop and have it go continuously and rapping over it. In these days, hopefully you do more with it than just loop it. Break it up, change it up, whatever."

Pos: "We never thought we would bring in something new. There was something new there. From High School we knew we were different. People noticed how our difference was unique, and when we came out with 'Plug Tunin'' [their first single in '88] it had something there that people started to grab onto, so of course we knew that with the album, it would send some new kind of music to the ears out there."

"We met the Jungle Brothers at a show in Boston," explains Dove. "From there ideas just clicked together. We exchanged phone numbers and we became best of friends, close as brothers now. We are brothers. With A Tribe Called Quest we became affiliated with them through the same thing. Ideas and concepts seemed to click with all of us."

"We're just family," continues Pos, "that's all we are. All together we are considered the 'Native Tongues'. We're a family group. Together we're the Native Tongues, separately when we break up we become De La Soul, Jungle Brothers, Tribe Called Quest, Latifah.

"We surround ourselves with each other because we all are talented people. We usually have the same ideals that are usually going the same way and we thrive off each other. Whatever Afrika [Baby Bambaataa, Jungle Brothers rapper] does, I watch and learn and whatever I do, he watches and learns. In music, we go back and forth.

"It was in the back of people's minds but they never tried to do it, they never thought

they'd be accepted. We're like the dare-devils of rap, trying to do things that others never did and we pulled it off."

There has been something bothering Mace for a while now. He wants to make it perfectly clear: "We never did call ourselves the hippies of rap," he protests. But their press officer did, and the label quickly stuck. "Because of the flower girls, people just took it to an extreme. We aren't the hippies of rap, we just enjoy what we do and we do it well, so we get on doing it.

"The reason we use samples is not because 'Oh we're stealing this and we're going to make money off of it', we're just appreciating artists whom we loved when we were growing up. We take the best music from the best people and we try to make it better. We hope they would look at it like that and not like we're dogging around their creativity. We're just making it more than what it was."

"It's not as if we don't think about it," stresses Pos, "but we don't sit down and compare lyrics and plan it out. It goes to show you. When we write all of the songs, me and Dove never sit down and write our rhymes together. I've never said to him, my rhymes dealt with this, maybe you should write about this. He writes what he feels and I write what I feel and it fits together."

Dove agrees: "We shock each other sometimes when we go into the studio and it's my turn to get upon the mic and record my vocals. Pos will be in the other room and will say: 'Oh shit, what I've wrote is the same'. And that happens to me when I'm listening to him on the mic. We may tell each other to rhyme in this style or this pattern, but we never discuss what we put in our rhymes beforehand."

"You find a lot of common styles," Pos notices. "You find Salt-N-Pepa that sounds like a Run DMC with the intermixing of rhymes, which is the Kid-N--Play, and people who try to rhyme straight up where they have the last word to rhyme on the same thing. It's not like that with us; we like to break one verse into three different sections, where the first last word might rhyme, at the end of the rhyme, the last one will rhyme with that."

Dove: "It's more about constructing the rhyme style. Then what it's all about is making the words fit inside. Actually making a scheme of rhyme is easy."

"We've been asked to do a lot of educational stuff with rhyming for kids," reveals Pos. "We're supposed to be doing a project with [director] Tamar Hoffs. Her daughter is the lead singer in the Bangles, and we're supposed to be working in an educational programme with kids because kids understand some of the music from the album. A lot of kids can rhyme and like to play with words."

On the transition to the second album...

Pos: "It's hard for me to think of De La Soul as a fad. Our music takes no type of form. People can say there's a little bit of this or that in it. I've never seen anyone define our music. You can't define us from our clothes, people expect us to dress like a lot of things but we dress differently every time you see us. Everything we do takes no type of form."

"D.A.I.S.Y. means 'Da Inner Sound Y'all'

but a lot of people didn't focus on what it meant, the sound from within. And through the time of the 'Three Feet High And Rising' album we didn't toss it out of the window, we kept it up because that's what people were focussing on. It kept the public happy but not many people understood the true meaning of it. We stressed it a lot of times and towards the end of the album's run, people started to get what we were trying to say. But we decided that we weren't going to go with this crazy idea of messing up people's heads and them not understanding what 'We Fell Into A Bottle Of Plastic Shwingalokate So We Opened A Radio Station' [the original title for their sophomore LP] was all about, so we though, 'Let's just kill all of this!'

"All we ever planned to be was a regular group - a group of gifted kids doing what they love. I think people will have misconceptions about what 'De La Soul Is Dead' means [although they tried to make it explicit on the sleeve – three dead flowers in a pot tipped to one side]. It isn't saying we're breaking up, nor is it saying the group doesn't like what they're doing. It should really have been titles 'The D.A.I.S.Y. Age Is Dead' but we wanted people to know that the D.A.I.S.Y. Ages was De La Soul.

"It's also to do with the fact that 'Three Feet High And Rising' was explaining everything about De La Soul. But now De La Soul is out the picture, and this album is describing everything we've seen – in our audience, on the road, the public's actions. This time it's the reverse situation – De La Soul isn't on the stage now, the whole

★ **Posdnous (left) and Trugoy The Dove take the DAISY Age to the stage**

crowd is on the stage and we're letting you know what we've seen."

On the 'Ring, Ring, Ring' single...

Pos: "We went over to Europe last summer, heard the [Curiosity Killed The Cat 'Name And Number'] single and liked it a lot. We thought 'We've got to use the chorus, it's real cool', and just decided to build a whole idea around it.

"At one time, we all had the same phone answering machine and it had there was a code on the answering machine – a manufacturer's code and we couldn't make our own – and every time we'd sit at the house and the answering machine would come on – someone was breaking this code of our answering machine to find out what our messages were! We just got fed up with it – so we wrote a song about it!"

And Curiosity's reactions?

"I'm not sure, but I think that Curiosity heard about our idea and thought it was kinda cool," he smiles. "As long as it's cool with them!"

"We had some trouble here and there [with sample clearance], but the way I see it now everything's practically clear," says a relieved Trugoy. "We're not going through any lawsuits anymore, not after our first album."

De La Soul were sued by '60s group The Turtles for use of a sampled drum break on 'You Showed Me' from 'Three Feet...'. Second time around they side-stepped injunctions by getting sample clearance from all concerned artists. It proved a lengthy process, delaying the LP by over a year.

Pos: "We had a new producer this time around, by the name of Double B and he gave us more of a street type of sound. We've been on the road with him for the last year now, and his own crew have got stuff coming out on Prince Paul's label [Paul, a former member of Stesasonic, was the production maestro behind 'Three Feet...'. Now a member of The Gravediggaz]. This time we produced most of the album. It's a different De La Soul.

Trugoy: "When people hear this album, I think they'll say 'These guys have changed as people'. We haven't changed – every song that we rap on, we are playing a character, somebody we saw while out on the road. The song called 'Afro Connection' is a high-five from a hoodlum's point of view. We went to towns like Chicago, Detroit, Washington and we saw this hoodlum attitude – so we're talking about standing on the corner selling drugs, or about getting upset at the cops watching you all the time, and a lot of people are going to think we're not the same happy-go-lucky guys we used to be. We are – we're just playing characters we see throughout the whole album.

"I always liked the groups where you didn't know what to expect next. The street kids are really going to like this album a lot, but they won't realise for a while that it's them we are describing. But we're just describing what we see. We hope that the real dedicated, happy-go-lucky fans don't reject it 'cos this is just role playing. But what we say had to be said.

"'My Brother's A Basehead' [crack/cocaine addict], that is a true story. As time goes on, people will understand whose brother we're actually talking about.

We've always said we like to mix humour into a serious topic so it catches the attention – the humour does that but there's always a serious and positive ending in it, from which people can learn."

On the state of hip-hop...

Trugoy: "I wasn't raised on music, I was raised on art! So the card really flips when it comes to me – I'm not the one with the record collection in the house, and I didn't get into music until I was in the sixth grade. I didn't concentrate on what jazz was, what R&B was, so I wasn't influenced by any particular kind of music.

"It seems a lot of groups are moving into the jazz realm – Q-Tip [A Tribe Called Quest] is about to go crazy with the jazz stuff – but it's one of those things that has been lame about rap. Once a new era starts, everyone starts to capitalize on it and see who can get the best loop. We never thought about that, 'cos as soon as Q-Tip came in he found a lot of groups – there's a group called Leaders Of The New School who've got some jazz stuff, Black Sheep have got some jazz stuff. We didn't jump on that, we just stuck to the De La sound...whatever that is! Gangsta rap is cool, but NWA was the shit when they came out, then Ice Cube, now Geto Boyz...now they are talking about having sex with dead bodies and that's outrageous. The music is good, but some of the stuff is just too much, they take it to an extreme. I know the streets and they don't talk about nothing like that on the street, I wouldn't think anybody fantasises about that! You can talk about the shoot-out you saw last week and you can talk about your hoes, but dead bodies..?

That has to stop."

So what's currently spinning on the De La turntable?

"Rap that is coming out now? A lot of it is basically garbage. Most of what I listen to now is not even rap – Anita Baker, Sade, Suzanne Vega, Phil Collins. When I do listen to rap, I listen to one of those compilations from '80-'81, or Run DMC's first album, stuff like that. Kids who go to work and make their 80 dollars a week figure they can put out a record on a small label – and they can – but taking your time means you put out a better product and there's no point in rushing your album out in a month. Too many people just want a record out with their name on it and they're not interested in making music – they're coming out with garbage work.

"It's not only the artists, it reflects onto the crowds. People aren't turning up to see shows 'cos they just don't want to hear rap anymore – rap itself. I'm disappointed that too many artists are just sitting back, 'cos it's hurting them and it's hurting rap. But hopefully groups like De La Soul, the Fam'Lee can stick it out for a couple more albums, or just infinity – whichever comes first!"

On fame, fortune, and the third album...

"Musically, I would describe De La Soul as geniuses!" says Trugoy with a straight face. "Sometimes I think the group is a little afraid to do what it really wants because we're afraid people won't understand. And it's sometimes because the group is lazy! 'Three Feet High And Rising', on stage, in front of cameras...it could have been better."

"It just flew like that," recalls Pos, looking studious behind a pair of large glasses. "It's not as if we were that off the wall. A lot of people were doing the same thing as each other. We're just one of those groups that could be down with using different things and incorporating what we like regardless if that's going on or not."

Trugoy: "A lot of times, when we had the chance to meet other rappers who were 'in' at the same time as us, they'd be like 'Oh, you used that type of loop; I was going to use that but I didn't think it would work for me'. A lot of rappers could've had the ideas, but they put themselves in a cage where they were restricted, where they didn't want to go further."

"Nah," says Pos. "People can be like 'I know you started this'. Whether we did or not, it really doesn't matter to us because we don't do what we do to get a pat on the back. We just try to come up with the best music we can and be as creative as we can."

"Everything we did was intentional," explains Dove. "To me the first album would've been the same way if there wasn't a 'Me, Myself And I' on there, regardless of how critically acclaimed it was and how good people thought it was. It would've never have sold as many copies if it didn't have a good, radio-friendly hit, which 'Me, Myself And I' was. So if we'd had a 'Me, Myself And I' on 'De La Soul Is Dead' we wouldn't even be hearing people saying 'Your album didn't do as good'. It was just as clever as the first album and it was what we wanted to do."

"To be blunt about it, we really don't care [about criticism]," Posdnous says nonchalantly. "All this time, from the beginning, when they said we were great, we always showed that we didn't care. We didn't make 'Three Feet High And Rising' to get a Grammy. We did it because of what was in us – and that's what really matters. Once we accomplish something that's beautiful, it's on to the next. As rappers we remain real to ourselves and humble. We ain't sitting here saying 'Oh yes, we are this' so when it's time to kick us down we're falling. We ain't falling, we didn't care about it."

"It was just amazing for us that we made the first album," continues Pos. "We'd never been to London or not even all over the States and for so many people to react to it, yes, that was amazing! Not the hype, but that all these people were reacting to these three kids they knew nothing about. But the hype – it wasn't as if we sat up there and let it go to our heads. That's why with the second album, when people didn't know what was going on and the hype wasn't really in our favour..."

"They think that we're constant laughter kids and we come cracking jokes," says Dove. "We're people – people have different emotions. One day we may be mad, one day happy, one day silly and one day serious. People misinterpret what they hear on wax. It is truthful but it's only a section of our lives."

"We look back as long as we've been in rap and it seems like now it's in the best state for us," adds Dove, fiddling with his cap. "What is underground is now mainstream. You're mainstream when you say 'I'm underground'... I think it's going to be the same for us as it's always been, but just to the side. It seems like nowadays that it's just all about a typical beat, with a bassline and horns over the top and everyone's talking about hanging out, smoking, girls and partying. Just basically a big party in the streets. We're not coming across that way and our music's not coming across that way. It's just as with the first and second albums, we're going to have our space on the side."

Pos adds: "[Success] is not the best thing in the world. I mean it's cool in the beginning when it's a new thing to you, but in time, as an individual it's a maturity thing too. Some people grow more quickly than others and in time you realise it isn't the greatest thing in the world. It takes away from your own personal life. Sometimes I think being behind the scenes is much more comfortable."

"It hasn't changed us," smiles Dove. "Faced with different situations, you realise what you're capable of and how you're capable of going into it and thinking your way out of it. It hasn't changed us, it just made us know who we really are.

"We're three individuals. We have the same feelings about things, but on a personal tip, we do our own thing. I myself stay in the house and we all have families, we have children. You got your girl on the side and you got to take care of business at home," says Dove, as Mace erupts into giggles!

Dove: "We were happy the way it ['Buhloone Mind State', 1993] was received. It kind of shocked us at how quick the fame came and how quick the acceptance came. When we first came out with 'Plug Tunin'', it was kind of iffy. We were wondering if they were going to like it. And when it was

accepted it was still not clear what was going to happen. And when something like 'Jenifa Taught Me' came out, it was like that more or less reinforced our feelings about what we had to do, so we came out with 'Three Feet High And Rising'. It was like, 'We're doing it our way regardless of the fact of what's out there, because they've accepted the previous things so let's do it our way. We went into the studio and did it just the way we wanted to, whether it was the best thing or the worst thing. And the album was great.

"When it came out, we got so many rave reviews, not just from magazines and stuff like that, but from our peers – from the rappers. Every club we went to, we would see a Kane or a Kid-N-Play, or a KRS-One, or a Salt-N-Pepa, or a Jazzy Jeff & Fresh Prince...whoever it may have been, they were coming to us giving us our props. That felt good. The album was just so comfortable, we were just so pleased about what we'd done.

"I don't see any flaws with the album itself. But we should have done what we wanted. A lot of people took advantage of what we were doing and how fast it was coming. And they made a lot of decisions for us..."

Dove: "A lot of people made a lot of decisions for us and we were new to it. And it was like, 'If that's what you think's going to make it happen, it'll happen'."

Pos: "We didn't know what it was to get burned. Now we know, so we're not hearing nothing like it..."

Dove: "I think that's the only flaw that we had. Now we go with our instincts and stick with our instincts." ■

3

dr dre

A founder member of both the World
Class Wreckin' Cru and NWA, Dre is
often referred to as the Godfather of
West Coast gangsta rap. After the
demise of NWA he continued to wield a
massive influence on the West Coast
scene, both as a producer (for the likes
of DOC, Snoop Doggy Dogg and Lady Of
Rage) and as a rapper in his own right;
his first solo album, 'The Chronic', was
released in 1993. Always a controversial
figure, Dre has left the angst and
acrimony of NWA behind him and
evolved into a fully-blown multi-media
personality. His fusion of gangsta lyrics
and laid-back, P-funk style grooves has
been stunningly successful, while a
spectacular solo video-clip won him an
MTV Award in 1995.

★ dr dre

"Back in the days of NWA, it was just a learning experience. I was just dropping a loop and putting a rap on it. With 'The Chronic' [the title is derived from a particularly strong brand of marijuana – the '90s gangsta rapper's drug of choice] I sat down and came up with the concept and thought how I wanted it to sound. A lot of people are into CDs right now, so that's why the clarity on the albums that I've done lately sounds so good, 'cos I take a lot of time with the sound.

"And from what I'm hearing, it's had a lot of influence 'cos a lot of shit coming out now has my sound on it. I hear a lot of people with the high-pitched melodies and shit, but it's only a compliment."

Released on Dre's own Death Row label, 'The Chronic' paved the way for the dominant 'G-Funk' sound of the West Coast – itself derived from the '70s funk of George Clinton and Funkadelic, and often recreated using a full studio band. It signified a definite progression from his early sonic sculpting with NWA, which owed more to the harder, frenetic sounds of early electro.

"Everybody in the business has been stepping to me: Michael Jackson, Madonna – she called me for about a week trying to get me to produce some stuff – but I had to turn them down. Sometimes you can hurt yourself like that. You take this amount of money now, and it can fuck you up later down the road. Right now I'm just about self and family – when I say family I mean people who are part of the organisation. I'm only doing material for Death Row. Why should I make someone else some money? And I don't wanna spread my sound out; I want it to be whenever you hear something from Dr Dre it's gonna be special. With my shit you never know what I'm gonna do next. I want Death Row to be like the Motown of the '90s. There's still a lot of things I wanna do."

On talk of an NWA 'reunion'...

"There was never gonna be a NWA reunion. It was just me and Cube. We were in an interview clowning around, and that came out and the next thing you know it's in every fucking newspaper. That the album was gonna be Niggas Without Eazy. But there was never any reunion planned or nothing like that. We're gonna try and get Ren on a couple of songs, but there was never any talk of a NWA reunion.

"Me and Cube have always been cool. We said something about him and he came back with his record; but there wasn't no real beef. As a matter of fact, we went out one time and he told me what he was gonna do. I was like 'Okay, whatever'. Like the beef with Luke [aka Luther Campbell, founder of the Miami-based 2 Live Crew]. We were working on the song 'Dre Day' and a friend of mine came into the studio and said 'Luke said this and Luke said that about you'. So I said 'OK, we need a third verse'. So that's how that came about. But I'd never even heard the record. To this day I've never heard the record he dissed me on. But I talked to him on the phone and he was telling me the same thing. 'I got something for your ass,' and that kinda shit, but there's no real beef between me and him."

And what about Eazy-E?

"Well, that's a bit more serious, but as far as I'm concerned it's all behind me. I'm just gonna get on with my life. Let him do his thang. I'm a do my thang. I'm not making more records about him. I made all the money I'll make on him so that's that. He can make a million records about me if he wants to; he's keeping my name out there, I couldn't give a fuck."

As house producer for Eazy-E's Ruthless label, Dre recorded eight albums (seven of which went platinum) but, like Ice Cube before him, split acrimoniously over alleged underpayment. His aired his discontent publicly in the LP track 'Dre Day' and its subsequent video. However, both Dre and Cube instantly squashed their beef to appear at Eazy's hospital bedside, when he was diagnosed as having full-blown Aids. He died, tragically, a few days later on March 26, 1995.

Apart from Death Row Records and his production duties, Dre has other projects he wants to get involved with. He has got more involved in the visual as well as the musical side.

"I've directed most of Snoop's videos. Back in the days when we were NWA, we used to sit down with a director and tell him all our ideas, on how we wanted the video to go, and he would just use our ideas and put them on film. So I decided to cut out the middle man and just do it myself."

Now Dre has decided to turn his visual creativity to a larger format.

"Me and my boy DOC are working on a movie right now, and my next solo album is gonna be the soundtrack to that. We just finished the first draught of the script. It's either gonna be called Root Of All Evil or One Time – that's a term we use in LA for the police."

And will Dre be shipping the script to the film companies? Nope, he's got that covered too.

"We started our own film company, Death Row Films. Right now I feel like there's nothing I can't do." ∎

4

gang starr

The pairing of Guru Keith E with DJ Premier should have been short-lived; it was a marriage arranged by a record company, and for the first few months of its existence the two worked hundreds of miles apart. Yet Gang Starr endured to become consistent purveyors of melodic, thoughtful yet hard-edged rap. Their first album, 'No More Mr Nice Guys', won them respect from the rap fraternity, while follow-up 'Step In The Arena' saw the introduction of what was to become the group's musical trademark: hardcore rapping over jazz breaks, beats and loops. Subsequent albums 'Daily Operation' and 'Hard To Earn' have affirmed the durability of Gang Starr, despite – or because of? – its members' deep involvement in solo projects.

★ gang starr

"Carlos told me about Wild Pitch Records," recalls Premier. "But I didn't think they could do anything for me since they were a little label. But they liked my stuff and they signed me immediately, but they didn't like our rapper. So I went back to Texas after the summer, and had to tell the group [Inner City Posse] that I got signed, but they didn't. I tried to explain it in a nice way, and the other guy said, 'This stuff's not workin'. I'm going into the Navy'. And the next day he was gone, out of school and everything!

"Then I had to ring Wild Pitch and tell them I had no rapper, and about the same time Guru Keith had all the trouble with his crew [Also called Gang Starr but then featuring rapper Damu D-Ski and DJ Wanna Be Down]. He'd heard my tapes and the label suggested that we try something together to see if it worked."

Prior to Gang Starr, Guru (Keith ALlam) was born and raised in Roxbury, Massachussets but moved to Brooklyn after attending college in Atlanta and working as a counsellor in a Boston maximum detention centre. Premier (Chris Martin) actually hailed from Brooklyn, but was studying in Texas when their partnership was cemented.

"Basically, the first album, 'No More Mr Nice Guy' (1990), was a test to see if we could cut it together; everything turned out cool, and we had the album written before I came back from my summer break. We recorded that LP in 10 days on my summer holiday.

"Basically, you can't take kindness for weakness. We do a lot of positive messages in the records, at the same time we're saying you can't be nice all the time. When you have a sucker that wants to play you out just because of the way you're being nice, there is a limit to being nice sometimes."

On the making of 'Jazz Thing'...

Often credited with spawning the jazz/rap genre, 'Jazz Thing' brought the duo into the limelight, a direction they capitalised on with the 'Step In The Arena' (1991) LP and Guru's solo 'Jazzmatazz' projects. An early version of the track was picked up on by prominent black film director Spike Lee, who asked his musical director Branford Marsalis to track the group down.

Guru: "Branford respected us as young artists, he had respect for rap music. He brought me a poem from Lotis Eli about the history of jazz. It was a long poem, and a lot of the lyrics didn't have that rhythm, so I adapted it to the beats that Branford and Premier put down. The best part of it, was that I realized that jazz evolved out of the street and social conscience – and that's where rap is at. Rap is here to keep bringing people back to remembering the old things."

For Premier it was a more lasting experience: "Branford played me the track and gave me the basic idea on how he wanted it to come out. He said I could change it however I wanted to. Next day I came into the studio with all my stuff and I fused my stuff into it. He had these modern sounds in it that didn't go with rap music at all. We ended up hanging out together, and he had never been to a hip-hop club before, so Keith E and I took him to Club Quando in Brooklyn, and he had never seen anything like it before. We introduced him to some of our friends and took him over to our place, which is really small. Once I took him around to see how we lived, he started understanding where we were coming from and we liked each other more. He gave me the freedom to express my ideas, and the music got more intense. Then Keith E changed all the lyrics, and we put together four different mixes so they could release it as a single off the soundtrack [to 'Mo Better Blues'], and we called it 'Jazz Thing'."

On writing for 'Daily Operation'...

Gang Starr's third album, '...Operation' marked a move away from its jazzy predecessor – back to the hardcore pastures of their debut.

Premier: "We usually sit around the house and we come up with a subject that we like to hit upon. We write it down, and then we start structuring it in our mind. Then I usually lay down tracks and music that sort of fits the titles, or I'll play a string of grooves to Keith, and then he'll decide which ones he wants to use for which subject."

Guru: "I write about everything we see in the New York streets. The last album didn't have any songs about girls, and on this one we've written a few, like 'Love Sick', about a particular instance that happened to me. I also wanted to come off with a different perspective on this album, I don't like to do too much rhyming stuff, instead everything is much more elaborate. My raps are like facilities – facts and realities of what's goin' on. Premier gives me the beats, but I've got a lot to say...

"The market is over-saturated and it's time for the real cream to rise up. If the cream can't rise 'cos it's being held back then it's time for us to take our spots.

"We'd come down from the studio right to the parking lot and if it sounds good in Premier's van, then the mix must be cool y'know? This album does have the Gang Starr flavour, the Gang Starr mystique, but it's more in your face.

"Have you heard KBS's 'Sex And Violence'? It's a similar thing with us;

going back to the raw stuff. Over here on the East Coast, the vibe is different. We don't have to talk about gangbanging and stuff 'cos we don't have gangs, when rap started there wasn't any gangs, so we just talk about what's going on in the ghettos of New York and the flavour is different.

"We wanted to bring the territorialism back because all these West Coast guys are talkin' about where they're from. It's not really a battle thing, it's just to let them know, and let the people in New York know, that we're proud of Brooklyn."

On mixing and marketing...

"The record company constantly stresses that's [a different mix] what they want in Europe, but when we play out there we play our versions and the crowd love it," says Premier. "We'll play remixed versions if they're slammin' but...so far I ain't heard any! I don't hate the people who do it, I just think the industry don't know how to market the rap like it is. But if you don't know how to market it, then why mess with it? The real stuff should prevail."

Guru: "It's no problem for me to rap with a live band as long as it's funky, as long as it's tight – as long as it sounds like a loop! That's how the Brand New Heavies are. The stuff they play sounds like the stuff we sample.

"It's cool for some people to rap with live bands but personally...well, I feel uncomfortable doin' that."

"We want to keep it like it was back in

the days," Premier continues, "turntables, mic, and rockin' it straight up live. It's all in the rhythm of your hands, and if you've got that and people want to hear the rhymes you kick, then that flavour is all you need. Some people need more to make their show carry, but we've got the energy to deliver straight-up."

"What we're gonna do is something hype," the Guru concludes. "We're gonna have such a phat sound system, big lights, and we're gonna bring you to the streets theatrically. I wanna bring in that rawness. It's time for real hip-hop to prevail."

On 'Hard To Earn'...

"To me, I think it's one of the best projects that we've ever done," Guru gushes about their solid fourth album, issued in 1994. "We both really put a lot into the making of it and it was just really cool getting back in the studio with Premier after doing all those separate projects. You know, there was rumours going around that we'd broke up, so we're gonna just catch chumps sleeping, 'cos when it comes out all our diehard fans are gonna be like 'Yes! They did it again! They didn't let us down!'. It's a phat record that's representative of what Gang Starr has always been doing, which is giving you the real stuff – a rapper and deejay with pure skills!"

"With 'Jazzmatazz' [Guru's solo project, a fusion of his raps and freeform jazz], there was no attempt by me to sell out. All I did was something that I felt was culturally important. When I put it together I didn't sit down and say 'Hey, I want to make something radio-friendly' or 'I wanna cross over to the jazz crowd'. I just did it 'cos it meant something to me. A whole lotta rappers now are just deliberately trying to achieve mass appeal.

"You know, I've always said my trademark is just my voice and one thing that I can claim – and I'll say this to any rapper's face – is I believe I got more styles than almost anybody! If you take all the music outta every album I've ever done, there's all kindsa different rhythms and vocal patterns, 'cos I write to the beats!

"It's weird because a lot of my rhymin' is message-related, but I disguise it. I go in and out of freestyle and sorta put it together into one. That's always been my thing, so it's a real spontaneous feeling that you get from listening to it. Like we got this one called 'Tons Of Guns' which covers the whole problem with guns in our communities, especially in the States – just talking about the problems and how people are dealing with it. The refrain is, 'What the fuck you gonna do in a situation/It's like you need to have steel just to feel the relaxation' and, you know, that's the truth of the matter. The other day I saw this show on TV where this lady had a line of clothing for people who carry guns – serious! Then the song 'Code Of The Streets' is another one that's definitely message-related. The first verse deals with how kids have peer pressure and then at the end it's like

'Hey, another court case/But it's the code of the streets'. It's basically saying 'Hey, this is what's really going on – brothers ain't trying to change'. You know, us brothers who are always in the news, we ain't the only ones doing crime, organised crime's been doing stuff for years. That street shit, man, it's important to me. That shit is real and we're gonna really go into these concepts on the videos and try to make 'em really phat! That's what this whole '94 Gang Starr thing is about; the street vibe of Gang Starr is the nucleus of everything I do – you know 'Jazzmatazz' was just a branch from it."

On the art (and politics) of sampling...

Premier: "I try to make everything different. Even though I do sample from other people's records, I still try to make it original in the way I back it up; that's why what I'd do say for Nas [Premier produced several tracks on his acclaimed 'Illmatic' debut in '94] I'd never do for Gang Starr, 'cos the artists have different ways of expressing themselves! See, with Gang Starr, that's more like our thing – it's our baby and our marriage whereas with everyone else I guess it's sorta like having an affair, and when you're married to somebody you know 'em way more than you know somebody you're having an affair with! I mean, then you're just getting a thrill for a little while, whereas the marriage keeps on going and there's more things that you know about each other! So no matter who I work with, I still love working with Guru the most, just because of the fact that our recording techniques have always worked and we just know how to bounce off each other without any problems.

"If I step in the studio with Guru he'll be there to do his vocals, and then he'll go about the rest of his business knowing that he can trust me to do everything else as far as mixing the record and all that, because that's how much confidence he has in me doing it! It's not that the other artists don't, but it's just that we have that type of marriage where we automatically know how we're gonna do everything. If somebody said that they need us to so a song today for a movie or something, all we have to do is know what it's about, and we can knock it out in one day! We don't hang that much personally, but when it comes to a recording we always got it going on...

"While I'd like maybe to get into using instruments in some of my outside production work, when it comes to Gang Starr – being that we do straight-up hip-hop albums – we'll stick with the traditional way of doing those type of records, which is the art of sampling

"I mean, sampling is an art form to me, but you have to know how to sample to make it artistic! And because anything that you consider art has also to be creative, it means that I like to be creative with what I use – even if it's just a James Brown loop!

"You know, back in time when hip-hop was just known on the streets and it wasn't a big business, nobody was giving a fuck about nuttin' as regards to sampling, whether it was James Brown

or anybody else. But when it got to the stage where money was involved and it blew up into this multi-million dollar type business, everybody started coming out saying 'I should get a piece of that!'.

"To a certain degree I agree that people should be paid, but it really depends on what's being used. I think if it's a hit record and it made a lotta money then of course it should be compensated for. But if it's just one little horn blast of something, there's still really no need to come out with that, just for the fact that it's like piecing a puzzle together – you know, finding a piece from all different types of areas in order to create one central thing. But, having said that, although this is probably the most unidentifiable album we've made, in terms of the basis of the music and the beat, we've definitely cleared everything! You know, just to be safe – it's like putting on a condom!

"Like the Ohio Players, who I'd never have sampled just for the fact of how big they are that I'd have to have got clearance! I've even sampled some George Clinton stuff this time, which is definitely unusual for me since the West Coast is so dominant in using him. But then you have to remember that the East Coast loves Clinton and Parliament too, it's just that we're not so much into preserving a particular style and not taking it any further ahead. You know, being as it started in New York, New York will always be ahead in terms of moving on and trying new things. New York artists like to keep taking hip-hop to another level and so, no matter how many records we may sell, we're still gonna always be ahead of our time here."

On East Coast v West Coast...

"You still got the East Coast and West Coast style being very different," argues Guru. "But now on the East Coast you got this thing where the groups tend to have gimmicks in order to sell a lot, which is completely different from the way Gang Starr has always been. Onyx, Das-EFX, Naughty By Nature – I love 'em all, but each one has come up with something that was sort of sloganish or gimmicky in terms of a look or a vocal style that stood out. And the reason they have to do that to succeed is to offset the fact that the West Coast has all this gangsta rap that's been commercialised by all those movies with the gangs and the drive-by shootings.

"None of that lifestyle compares to life in Brooklyn or in the Bronx. I mean, a 13-year-old kid in the Bronx might walk around strapped everyday and he ain't in no gang – he just might be by himself sticking up other kids. Or there might be this kid whose name is known for nobody to fuck with because he got eight or nine murders to his name, which is called 'catchin' bodies' and is like a cool thing to brag about. That's how it is on the East Coast. No gangbanging, it's all about survival!

"The only way you join another guy is that you can make money together – not for the honour or the colour or the 'hood! Plus, it's less out than out West, so you

don't live in a 'hood, you hang with the kids from your block! And because I wanna get into some acting in the future, I been telling a lotta film makers: 'Do something about the East Coast, with some East Coast rappin' in it, so that it offsets what's going on, and then the sales will be more even'. Like on Juice they tried to do it, but the slang was all wrong and we don't have things like deejay contests where deejay's wear cut-off gloves or whatever. That movie was inconsistent and it's really now just a question of letting people see what we represent a little more!"

On DJs v live bands...

"Some people go with bands, some people just go with the traditional turntable – everybody can't be the same," Premier begins diplomatically. "But regardless of whether you're with a band or not, I always think that the turntable should be one of the instruments that's on stage, 'cos that's what started this music! If it wasn't for Kool Herc [the street deejay who pioneered the art of sampling in the early '70s] and all of 'em bringing it back and forth and cutting, doing the scratching to repeating and keeping a record going on the same break, then it would never have got to the stage where someone would pick up a mic to rock a party!

"I stay focussed completely and I think a lot of deejays need to be like me and get into production! I mean because deejays are the ones that pick the records that are actually played, they should also be

★ **Guru (centre) experiences a new reality as Jazzmatazz goes live**

capable of making tracks that other deejays wanna play! You know, there's some deejays whose only way of making a living is just spinning for somebody and I think they should take it to another level, because if I just deejayed I wouldn't make anywhere near the money that I make! Also, by getting into production you become even more important in your own group because your extra skills gives you more involvement. That's why I have just as much input into Gang Starr as Guru does, because I don't just come in there to do scratches – I actually lay all the tracks!"

On the 'Jazzmatazz' project...

Guru: "I try to stay on the cutting edge because there's so many people making hip-hop these days. I always try to be original and different. And now the 'Jazzmatazz' thing is almost like a whole new sound: the way I do certain tracks now, I could use 'Jazzmatazz'-style production for other artists. It just has to do with the way the East Coast tracks are developed: the dirty beats, a dirty bassline groove and a drum – you start out with something raw and come out of that with some live music. And it's funny because the whole style of rap now is coming out with more live music, more vocalists are being used, there's more music, so it's right on time with what's happening.

"It's called 'The New Reality' [released in 1995, the second of Guru's 'Jazzmatazz' sets]. It's like this: negativity is a chronic disease. I'm the cure causing infections to freeze. It's about everything that's going on in my life and in the world."

He picks up the track listing and points out how the album is divided into four thematic sections of four songs each, and how there is a 'jazzalude' to introduce each section.

"The 'jazzaludes' are the themes for the four songs that follow it," he explains. "Jazzalude one is 'New Reality Style'. Jazzalude two is 'Defining Purpose', three is 'Hip-Hop As A Way Of Life', four is 'Maintaining Focus'. It's a little lifeskills type of thing. This shit is about living, straight-up, the shit is real...

"If I've got a cool uncle that's 50-something years old, he could be the coolest motherfucker and I could jam with him. That's what it's about. Or if I know a female singer, hey, we can get together and jam. It's a family thing, man. That's all it is. The older jazz cats that we sampled from for so long, we're bringing them to life; letting people see who they really are. And we're letting the older crowd know that rap music isn't just a bunch of violent noise; that it's essential; that it's a tool; that it's a safety valve for society.

"There's Donald Byrd, Bernard Purdie, Ramsay Lewis..." he gestures as if to say 'the list goes on'. "...These are the coolest cats, man. The knowledge of life they have is invaluable. If I can sit down and talk to a guy like that about music, about life, for half an hour, I don't care, I know I'm gonna learn something. For me it's been great. It's cost me a lot of money to do this album, but it's been worth it for the experience.

"I talked with Donald Byrd; from day one he's been down with the concept, and we talked about the lack of unity, the black family, the black community, things that are important. How the older people are afraid of the youth, and the young people don't have that much respect for the older people. And how that's just because of things over the years being systematically divided. Poor employment structures, poor educational structures."

In discussing these issues, Guru was able to show his jazzateer colleagues how modern rap is a way of bringing such complex ideas into people's consciousness:

"We just built on those things, and we just vibed and agreed on a lot of stuff. And he was like, 'Rap is necessary, it's history, it's literature'.

"It's funny, a lot of those same musicians who were cynical have changed their views. Some still haven't, but I'm not working with the ones who haven't. Why would I work with someone who can't release? I'm working with the hip, so to speak, and they view the young generation as something that's vital.

"What's wrong with me jamming with guys we listen to anyway? That's the whole concept. It's the family vibe. You got the elders, you got the youth. It's a community. That's what 'Jazzmatazz' is to us, it's a community.

"These guys come to the sessions right on time, ready to play. They listen to the tracks ahead of time and they just get it done." After years of playing and touring, and often enduring a great deal of

hardship, these people are some of the greatest to work with, he says. "They live to play, that's what it is. They've got their people that they vibe with and they keep them going and that's a cool thing." And Guru is overjoyed that these musicians, with a clearer idea of what hip-hop is about, now feel a link to him:

"It's a blessing to me, as an individual, as I get older as I come up in this thing, to meet people like that. And now I have four or five albums behind me. As I develop I get wisdom, I get knowledge from brothers like that."

And how do they see him?

"I think they see me as someone who's trying to do something legit, and not follow any bandwagons. They know I'm not in it just for silly reasons...

"I did the rhymes last," he explains, "because I like to do the rhyme while the featured artist is there. That's the vibe that we create. I'm improvising my thing, and they're improvising theirs. Nothing was pre-written in my room or anything. All the lyrics were written in the studio. That's how I get my flow and that's how I start what I want to say."

On the 'Jazzmatazz' message...

"There's a lot of imbalances in society," Guru fumes. "Why is it that a guy who sits on the bench of a sports team is making four or five time the salary of someone who's gonna teach your kid or my kid in a city school in America? That doesn't make any sense. That's why those who are teaching are not really motivated. You and I could be really good teachers, but there's not enough money in it. It's fucked up because then people quit and they do other stuff; go into acting, writing music or whatever. The best teachers are usually people in the arts and too often they do something else. 'Cos teaching doesn't pay their rent.

"I was a rebel first before I became a teacher. I was a rebel with a cause. Not without. If something seemed wrong to me I would attack it. Some people out here don't have a sense of what's right and what's wrong; they just do dumb shit. The Bible says do unto others as you would have them do unto you. Every other holy book says things like that. But people don't live that way. Most people are living for today. People are not living for the future. They want it right now.

"A lot of older people don't realise they could save a lot of lives if they had a little bit more concern. And understanding. If they took a little more time. Because people reject the youth; they don't understand their energy. There's energy that can be channelled properly by properly educating them. You can't be just, 'Get out of the class because you're being disruptive'."

On the future of hip-hop...

"If I thought it was played out I wouldn't do it. But I can do something different with it every time. This is real music with real lyrics that are intense, from somebody with a world view and a dope philosophy that people need to listen to. I'm not out there grabbing microphones just saying nonsense.

"What I'm trying to do is something concrete and something with a vision. It represents the heart and soul of something.

"This is the ill funk, but it's taken form jazz-funk. Anything that makes you bob your head is funky, period. Whether it's jazz, rhythm and blues. If it makes you bob you head it's funky. And it's with that live element, but it's with that East Coast point of view. It's mad skills – no curses – something that a single mother that cares a lot about what her child listens to will say, 'I'm gonna get this.'

"So what I would like to see in the States is for this [the latest] album to be marketed in a similar way to a G-Funk album. It shouldn't be, 'Oh, we got this large crossover crowd' or nothing like that. Everything that's dope has to start from the street. And anything that's gonna last in rap has to start from the street. That's why I don't compromise on my beats, my lyrics, my concept.

"The chain and the star in Gang Starr represent the links that represent struggle: the unity amongst struggle and the power that comes out of that. That is the music. That is the star and that is the music. That is always the nucleus to anything that I do.

"'Jazzmatazz' is another aspect of me. It's a chance for me to do something solo, but the roots of it is the deejay and the family.

"So Gang Starr represents family to the youth out there trying to make it. All over the world in the street. 'Jazzmatazz' represents from the whole." ■

5

ice cube

A founder member – along with Dr Dre, MC Ren, DJ Yella and the late Eazy-E – of gangsta rap band NWA, Ice Cube quit the group after the release of their first serious album, 'Straight Outta Compton', in 1989. While the album sold millions, the band's confused stance on the issues affecting contemporary black America seemed to cramp Cube's style, and the man himself was destined for greater things. His hit single 'A Good Day' gained him crossover recognition; albums 'The Predator' and 'Lethal Injection' enhanced his reputation within the rap world; and he successfully branched out into music production, acting, and screenplay writing. Ice Cube gave his first interview to HHC just prior to his departure from NWA...

★ ice cube

On the origins of NWA...

"Dre's cousin used to live down the street from me. I used to live in Compton, but I moved to LA. I told Dre I could rap, but he already had a hook up for records through the World Class Wreckin' Cru. We became friends. I was writing some stuff and I started helping him on writing some the Wreckin' Cru projects. So when Eazy-E came along, he was a friend from our neighbourhood back in Compton, he was into something he didn't want to be into no more... He was doing something that he definitely needed to get out of. Dre said to him, 'Why don't you make a record?' Eazy said, 'Cool', but he's more a manager type of guy.

"He told us, 'I'd rather be the manager'. He had this group, but the group wasn't working out, and I had already written this song called 'Boys In The Hood'. The group he had – they wanted to do it but then Dre said to him, 'Why don't you do it? He had never rapped before in his life, but he did it and it jumped off. Eazy had his solo record and it was getting hotter and hotter. Then the groups we were

in messed up. The group Dre was in, he wasn't getting paid. The group I was in, I wasn't getting paid. We decided to make a record on Eazy's label, 'cos when he came out with his first record, he had it put out on his own label.

"The first songs all of us did together were 'Dope Man' and 'Eight Ball'. After that, the group was formed.

"With 'Boys In The Hood' we wanted to try a new style out. You know, talkin' about the real deal, about reality. A lot of people fake it, but we just wanted to come out with something real. With 'Dope Man' it was the kind of shit nobody ever heard on record.

"When you're in LA you just know gang members. Sometimes you run with them, sometimes you don't. Sometimes you get in trouble, sometimes you don't. I was never the type of person to join any one gang. If I wanted to hang with them one day, that's what I do. I go shoot some basketball, you hear what I'm saying? It isn't like I run with gangs. All the things we see on the street, nobody was rapping about. Every time we see California, it was a big cover-up just because all that the media was showing was Hollywood. And we was like, 'Yo, we got real problems out here and nobody wants to talk about them.'

"I'm not pro-gang, but when you're 19 and you're black and you dress a certain way, you get described as a gang member. Even if I'm not a gang member, I'm classified as one anyway, and that's a racist reaction to young black men on our streets. The police stop your car, they call you all sorts of names and make you get face down on the kerb. They'll do this to you for a long time, and at the end of it you won't even be given a ticket because you're clean. All that humiliation for what?

"Out here, black people are judged by the way they dress. White people are judged by their personality. That's how the system is. If there's a white guy who's 25 in a Mercedes Benz, he's probably a stockholder. A black person driving the same car must be a drug dealer.

"Let's not pretend. This is a white society. They may talk about equality, but it's not really equal because you don't see many white people in the ghetto. You only see black and hispanic minorities in the ghettos. When you look on TV, all you see are caucasian people. Yo, I'm like 'how can I be racist and I'm not even part of the majority'. I got my back to the wall and I'm the minority."

"Things are bad. I describe rap as the black kids' 'rock & roll', and the black kids' 'news network'. We take pains to rap about things that are mostly real things, and do happen. You might not see it every day. I might not see somebody getting shot every day, but I hear about it.

"Here's what I don't understand, that the city doesn't take any action to stop the violence. People are killed every day in black neighbourhoods, but once a white person is shot, that's when everyone starts making a fuss.

"It sticks out like a sore thumb. They put white police in our neighbourhood, knowing that they don't give a fuck. I'll tell you how the guys who are involved in gang activity are around here. They think if one of their homeboys got killed, they wouldn't call the police. That would be the last thing they do because they know all the police would do is take a report and that would be that. They'd rather take the law into their own hands.

"It's the Wild West out here. The police are here to protect, but who is protecting us from the police?"

On the accusation that NWA promoted violence...

"I don't promote shit. I'm just a guy making records. The only thing I want to promote in my life is me on this record making money. That's all I want to promote. That's all I'll ever promote. I'll continue this tale and tell

you what I see. They say it's negative, but if your learn something from it then that's positive. People are always going to down you, especially when you go against the grain. I don't want to be a role model and end up as a puppet.

"If I'm a role model and I didn't want to address the drug issue, I'd have to do something on drugs anyway. Maybe a role model wouldn't give a damn about the drug situation and they have to do something on it or talk about it because the public wants them to. I'm not that kind of guy to be told what to do, never was. I never did what teachers wanted me to do, unless I wanted to do it."

On the name 'Niggers With Attitude'...

"It just came to us all together. We had made up a list of names, but that was the name that had the most impact. That name hits you like a brick wall. What I don't believe is that people come up to me and say, 'Why you say nigger? Why don't you say brother'.

"I have to tell them, 'I ain't been saying brother'. Nigger is a word that we, black people, have been called and then we took it up. It's a word used in communication between people in our race. People say 'brother' in your face, but when they're with their homeboys they say 'nigger, please'. I ain't into that. I'm into being real on record and off record.

"New York is kinda crazy to me. Everyone there is on an African tip, but before you look at Africa, you got to look

at America. How am I going to look at Africa when our situation over here is so fucked up?"

On Compton, NWA's home town...

"It's a nice, peaceful neighbourhood in the daytime, but at night, that's when all the shit happens. A fox in sheep's clothing. There's Shooting, crack dealing, prostitution, all kinds of stuff. It's not that I hear up and down my street somebody got shot, but if you walk from my house to the store, which is three blocks away, you're putting your life in danger. Some fool in a gang swoopin' around the corner, you just take that chance. The chance you take when you leave your house at night, you don't know when they're going to start shooting.

"See, in New York, I rode the subway, walked from the subway to my friend's house and I'm a paranoid chicken; but we're walking at night, and everybody is out on the street? Damn. In LA, you don't see that. You might see people on busy streets because people rarely shoot on busy streets. But on a side street, nobody's there. Somebody dies in LA every night by shooting. Last year, 400 people died in and around Compton, and there are only 365 days in a year.

"If it wasn't for NWA and rappers like Ice-T, nobody would ever know that kind of stuff was going on in Southern California. That movie 'Colors' was only half the story. They fucked up 'Colors' because they showed it from the police's point of view. They should have showed it from a gang member's point of view or from someone living in the neighbourhood. NWA music, we do it from our point of view and they try to down it because they never put nothing in a black point of view unless it's good-time bullshit or some brother who says 'dy–no–mite'...

"Some of the shit is true. Black neighbourhoods *are* violent. Some black people are violent, but it is a small percentage compared to the good people. But people look at all our race as violent gangbangers and that puts the life of innocent blacks in danger.

"I'll never forget where I come from. Just because friends of mine are on the street doin' what they're doin', that doesn't mean I won't stop by and say, 'Y'all be coolin', watch what y'all doin', watch yourself, watch the police'. After that I keep going, because it's really none of my business. It's not up to me to act like somebody's father. 'Cos people always talk about our song 'Gangster, Gangster', saying that their little kid walks around rapping our lyrics.

"I have to say, 'Yo, if you let a rapper be a better role model than you, you're a bad parent'. Little kids look up to rappers, some kids want to be like you, but if you let your kids talk like a rapper, you're a bad parent. You're depending on us to raise your kids.

"Fuck that. I'm not no role model and I'm not a babysitter for no kids. I hear five year old kids saying 'fuck' and shit slipping out their mouths, but when we put that on record, we're not saying nothing that everybody doesn't know.

"We're not against the Self Destruction Movement or all of that. We just look at it as if that's a dream because we deal with reality. You can tell everybody to chill, but not everybody can rap. Everybody doesn't have it as good as KRS–One, or Kool Moe Dee or MC Lyte. Nobody has it that good. Down on the street, they have to make a livin', and they aren't all of a sudden going to say, 'Oh, man, I'm going to stop making my $400 a day, I'm going to try and get me a job'.

"They got to sit out there and make their money. I say this and it's cool to say it to a reporter, 'cos you seem to be able to understand, but when you say that to the world, that it's real and those guys out there have to make their money, people freak. We want life to be peaceful, but we know it won't be plain and simple. It's not a black situation, it's not a white situation, it's just a messed up situation."

On the split from NWA...

"It was between me and the management, y'know. I didn't like the management and I still don't. I think Jerry Heller's taking their money like he was taking mine. I wasn't down with that, so I left. Jerry Heller's gone and turned the guys against me.

"But I couldn't care less what another man thinks of me; it really don't matter because I'm a man and I've gotta make my own decisions."

On the spelling of 'AmeriKKKa' in the LP title 'AmeriKKKa's Most Wanted'...

"That's really what America is to me – a form of white supremacy. America wasn't built for me, it was built *by* me. When I say me I mean my race of people. All the baseball, apple pie and 4th July stuff, I don't feel that at all. It don't make no difference to me."

"I wanted people to get some kind of dimension on what's going on with me and how I felt inside about certain subjects that I couldn't do if I was in NWA. As far as 'Gansta's Fairytale', 'Turn Off The Radio', 'It's A Man's World' – with NWA I couldn't do those type of records.

"The record is more thought out because I was able to take my time. Some of the things on 'Straight Outta Compton' were spur of the moment things. Me, I had time, I had a year to sit back and observe and that's what I do best – just observe people. I look at a lot of news and a lot of what's going on and I don't go away from my neighbourhood. I'll have meetings all week but I'll cancel them just to sit in the neighbourhood and kick some rhymes with my homies... Just coming up with new material all the time.

"Someone who's making $100,000 or $200,000 a year can't tell the kids to stop selling crack or stop doing this. My view is this: what if you wasn't making records, what would you do? That's what I ask the rappers and that's how the kids look at it. I know a lot of rappers have good intentions but for me to stop doing what I'm doing's not gonna pay the fucking rent at all. Everybody can't rap so I don't chastise kids, I just give them the facts. As long as they know that they're making their own decisions – they know right and wrong – so I leave it at that. I'm not nobody's parents, I ain't here to raise any kids, I'm not into that. I'm into making funky music that kids can relate to and gain information from."

On the way forward for blacks...

"The way is to stop looking at white people as the enemy. That's the way for it to get better, to stop looking at them as the enemy but to just keep them out of our pockets. That's the worst way you can hurt somebody – to get them in the pocket.

"We need to start trying to develop our own black businesses, spend money with our own people and try and do what the Japanese do. They built their own fucking community – that's where they shop, where they spend their money and where they make their money. We need to do the same thing. I call it 'The White Out Programme'. Y'know, I've nothing against white people at all but I've gotta come up. America ain't shit and I've gotta get my chunk out of it. The real pimp is the motherfucking record companies, you know what I'm saying?

"The record company is the pimp, the artist is the ho, the stage is the corner and the audience is the trick. That's the thing man, they get all the money and I refuse to be a ho. I'm trying to get as much money out of these motherfuckers as I possibly can.

"I've got so many friends that died before they reached 21. I just reached 21, I thank the Lord that I was even able to. Black–on– black crime is imprinted in our minds, that we have to backstab each other to get over. Even in slavery time, you had blacks that work in the house and blacks that work in the fields. The ones in the field all wanna work in the house, right, so what they do to work in the house is expose the ones working in the house. It just came down from generation to generation where black kids don't have love for each other, they don't respect each other. What we gotta do is put the mirror on them and let 'em see all sides of each other so they can have some respect.

"To be honest, people can say I exploit the shit but they can do shit like 'Scarface' – put out movies and promote it on TV. When I do records that tells the truth these motherfuckers say 'he's part of the problem'."

On rap as a black news network...

"I kinda picked that up from Chuck and, when you think about it, it's true. You never have black news, you always have news *about* blacks. The only time you do see them is when they do something wrong. I can sit here right now with cable which has 63 channels – there's no blacks, no blacks... I'm flipping – no blacks, no blacks... I'm seeing a white face and I'm on 9 already... no blacks, no blacks, we can go on a little further... I'm on 23 and I haven't seen a black face yet. We just don't get to see our own images at home, what we see are white images all the time. I'm on 32 now, no blacks, no blacks, 37, 38 and now 39 – which is BET – Black Entertainment. Now I see a black face which is Ice-T rapping...

"Rap just helps kids to understand each other better, you know what I mean? I wanna see what the world would look like if it wasn't for rap. Rap put a lot of kids closer together. I didn't never know what was going on in New York and they didn't know what was going on on the West Coast so kids were further apart. Now it just puts everything together – you can see the same hairstyles in LA as you can in Alabama and all over the world. It's just putting people together so we all know the same things and we stop fighting each other and know what to fight against and what to fight for. It's the same shit all over the country, all over the world."

On his use of the word 'bitch'...

"It describes a particular type of woman, just as if you would say 'she's a queen', y'know what I mean? It's not degrading all women, it's degrading a certain type of woman. If I say 'bitch' and a woman feels insulted she should look at her own character because if she knows she's not a bitch it wouldn't affect her in any kind of way.

"A bitch is a bitch... A woman has a power with her body to get just about anything she wants from a male. Do you agree with me on that? Now, if she uses that power wrongly – just like if I use a gun wrongly I'll be called a criminal – if she uses her body to manipulate, to con and to steal, then she's a bitch.

"I'll put it like this – here's why a lot of crime happens in Los Angeles and around the country, around the world. There's a woman, right, and there's a guy. The guy wants the woman but the woman doesn't want the guy unless he has a fancy car or all the money. He can't go work at the fast-food restaurant – which are the only damn jobs we can get, it seems like – to get this fancy car. So what does he have to do? He has to rob somebody with the fancy car so he can get the money and get his own fancy car and then he can get the girl. This happens like every day. It happens a lot. Why do you think people want fancy cars and clothes? To attract the opposite sex, no other reason. I want to look good to the opposite sex, so I can *win* in life; so that's what everything boils down to.

"So you see the power that's there and when you use it wrongly you've gotta be deterred from that. My way to get girls from not having that attitude is to call them a 'bitch', and hopefully my peers will do the same and hopefully that will turn a lot of women around because they don't wanna be called bitches and they don't wanna be put in that category. So they turn their views around and hopefully they'll walk the right path.

"Anything you say can be taken the wrong way – anything. It happens with rap but singers, y'know, they talk about sex but very rarely do they talk about marriage *and* sex, so when they say 'turn off the light' – a kid can say 'well I can turn off the light with my 12-year-old girlfriend, y'know what I mean? But nobody hassles them about that. They only hassle the rappers 'cos the rappers get the records to the kids.

"As long as they hate me then the kids will love me. When the press start loving you too much and try to put you as a fucking role model and try to put you on commercials and shit like 'you're the best thing' – kids shy away from that shit.

"If I teach you something you don't know it's positive. If you learn from a good experience or a bad experience it's teaching you how to deal with that – so it's positive. If you burn your hand on the stove you hurt yourself – that's negative, but you know not to put your hand on the damn stove again so it's positive."

"If you listen to my songs and you say 'Damn, I did something like that and that shit was stupid. If I keep doing what I'm doing I'm gonna get caught one day'. Y'see the police can make a million mistakes but someone out there doing a crime can only make one.

"I consider myself an artist who talks about reality. I don't give a fuck how people want the world to be, I just tell them how it is.

"I'm gonna keep talking about things that are going on. If it takes me a while to come up with new material I'm gonna take that while 'cos I'm not gonna come out with something that's weak. I never stop writing. I'm trying to get my ideas together for the next record. The next record might go in a whole new direction.

"I ain't gonna try and rap forever. If I do another album that'll probably be it. I respect the kids and I respect the industry and they need to see new people. All this other bullshit is starting to get too commercial and I ain't with that. I think motherfuckers appreciate you more when you aren't always in their face."

On the 'Death Certificate' album...

"The album has a 'Death' side and a 'Life' side. The 'Death' side is the position of the black community all around the world, how we are now as far as the killing is going on, and the way we are thinking.

"The 'Life' side is where we need to go. There's records on there called 'I Wanna Kill Sam', like me searching out Uncle Sam for the things he's done to black people since we were brought over here 400 years ago.

"Then the album touches on the Korean problem we have in the community 'cos they're buying up on everything and they don't treat people with any kind of respect, so it deals with that. It deals with black people selling out themselves, their race, by trying to be something they're not. It deals with the gang problem – there's all kinda angles. It has a few twists in the tail. I think it's a much stronger album than 'AmeriKKKa's Most Wanted'. There's a progression in my work? Sure.

On editing the swearwords out of 'Dopeman' so his mum could listen to it...

"Well, my mom is my mom. She respects the views that I have and I teach her a lot of stuff about who she is.

"My mother willed me into existence, she put it into my mind, while I was still in her stomach, that I am not going to have to live through this. That's the reason I am the way I am.

"She's the first person who ever taught me anything. All the kids today, we ain't nothing but warriors but we just fighting the wrong war – the Government got us fighting against each other. They know if we turn and fight the real killer, they know they got a fight on their hands they just can't win.

"We've got to work, educate each other on who we are, and if they try to stop us – we're gonna go to war. If we try to educate our own and everything in this country is alright, why they trying to stop that? They have a plan to hold us and take us back. If we have a teacher they kill him!

"When you say Afro–American it's bullshit. We ain't Americans – we just lost what we are. It's time for us to put the ship back in motion and use any kind of media outlets and rap that we can – besides the paper interviews.

"Why? Because if I'm saying something too heavy the editor will edit it out. I'd rather talk to the kids through lectures, then none of my words can be censored. In 'Rolling Stone', I said a lot of stuff and they printed bullshit. What can I do? I'm dealing with all these bullshit reporters that don't wanna tell it just like I tell them.

"We gotta pool our resources to find entertainers who are on the same wavelength, who are not trying to be white, and then maybe we can do something...but now every time a brother makes some money he wants to get out.

"Some of the stuff [written about him] is cool, some bullshit – it's not dealing with the issues, it's just tenny bopper shit. I don't really read these interviews – I start, but they get too crazy..."

On gangsta rap and the 'Predator' LP...

"I wouldn't call what I do gangsta, because gangsta rap tends to be cartoonish. It's like a comic book. A lot of shooting, a lot of fighting, but you don't get nothing out of it. My raps are more reality-based because the things I talk about are true. I just don't talk about how many people I can shoot up, I deal with real issues. You can define the lyrics I do as reality-based, not gangsta...

"I want all my albums to have a different identity. After the things that happened in LA, a lot of people expected my record would be geared solely towards that. I already spoke out on those things that occurred in Los Angeles way before it happened. I talked on the problems that were going on, so it wasn't necessary to repeat myself. Anything you needed to know about, you just had to go to the Ice Cube Library to find out my views.

"I really wanted to do a record that was more geared towards hardcore hip–hop than towards a real political agenda. Even though I speak on certain topics that are politically oriented, and I don't think I can ever get away from that. I wanted to do something new. I don't want people to get an angle on me and say, 'Uh, we expect his record'll be like this'. Some groups you pick up their album and you know what to expect. But an Ice Cube record? I want people to say, 'Damn, he done it again. He fooled us again!' I don't want the media to be able to put an angle or label on me."

On the American political system...

"I believe in voting on a city level, for city officials you can walk up to and tell them your problems and what you expect from them. When it gets to the governors and senators, even the President, you can't walk up to them. That's why I don't believe in voting, unless it's on a small scale. When it's big, you can't express your opinions and it gets out of wack!

"No matter who's President, I think there's a certain amount of people that run this country and even a certain amount that always control the world. With things that big, the cries of the people are not heard. No President has ever had black people's interests in mind, they never tell blacks what they'll do for them specifically. It's just: 'Yo! Elect me and you'll be all right' and nothing gets done.

"Every four years we have hopes and dreams, but nothing ever gets done because we have to do for ourselves and I don't think a political candidate is going to help out our situation. We have to be willing to sacrifice to do it.

"This country is on the threshold. You see these things [public disorder and rioting] happening in more and more cities, more and more frequently. America is heading in the same way as Babylon and Sodom & Gomorrah. When wickedness over–powered the good, the nation always fell. And it's happening here.

"People are going to get really mad and want to know why they can't have food or money, when there's more than enough to go around. They're going to look to the politicians and see them as big fat cats feeding us bullshit. We are on the threshold of something. I'm just making sure I'm prepared."

On his Street Knowledge label...

"I'm real creative and I have to get the energy out, so the best thing for me to do is produce other groups. Unfortunately I can't release an album every six months. The best thing is to produce artists. It means I can do things outside Ice Cube, like Del Tha Funkee Homosapien and Yo–Yo, even Da Lench Mob. I also want to learn the business from the inside so I can soon distribute my own records. I want to gain a little insight into the business so I have something to fall back on when Ice Cube ain't in the spotlight no more.

"The whole thing is to keep the poor poor and the rich rich. The rich can't be rich unless the poor is poor. The rich control all the media outlet, movies, music, newspapers, magazines. Once you control all information you can swing people any way you want to. When we distribute information without going through the proper channels, they don't like that. Rappers, we make the music and we don't necessarily have to go through those channels to get exposed. There's no way to stop us. People are starting to think differently."

On communicating with the white population...

"There's a revolution going on in white households. Kids who used to listen to Stray Cats or Adam Ant, now they've got Ice Cube and Public Enemy posters. Their fathers are saying, 'Woah! What's going on? Why are you dressing like this? Why are you listening to that? 'And the kids are saying, 'Yo, we ain't rolling like you used to roll'. You know what I'm saying? 'You're the one that got America so fucked up in the first place'.

"I feel the kids are understanding. Or there wouldn't be the backlash from America over white kids buying rap music more than black kids. So if the music wasn't affecting who they are, America wouldn't attack rap music the way it is. So they are evolving into something new. And we are evolving into something new as well, by learning about ourselves and having pride in ourselves. White kids are like, 'What am I doing to keep this thing going, or am I doing anything to stop it? If I don't see myself in that song then I'm down and Cube's not talking about me'. Which I'm not, But if the shoe fits... you better check yourself. Definitely, before you wreck yourself."

On living the suburban life...

"Where I am now [in the San Fernando Valley], it's pretty cool. I got a nice quiet place. When I go out of town what I don't want to worry about is some fool going to come and kidnap my wife and family. It makes me focus, makes me say exactly what I got to say, because now I've got people behind me. I don't want my kids to have to go through what I went through. I want to see some justice in my lifetime, that motivates me more. And I'm less wild than I was when I didn't have kids. I can't go out there and get killed. Who's going to raise my kids? So when it comes to making that decision, should I go to this party or take my ass home, most of the time, I take my ass home.

On his future as a recording artist – and the future of blacks in America...

"If I ever make a record that doesn't sell a million copies, I'll stop. I will, I will stop. That's how it should be, if you ask me. Hip–hop's foundation is skills, you have to have skills on the microphone. Me, all I used to do is rap. Now it's a business and I don't rap for fun much any more. But you got kids out there, man, all they do is rhyme and do beats. So if you don't keep in contact, never put yourself on a level where you can't go down and freestyle with some kids, you'll lose it. That's why I always use different producers. Nobody ever has seniority

over me. They always have to work for me. If this kid I met yesterday has better beats than someone who I've been working with for five years, I'll go with the kid. The only thing constant about my records is me. I always have control. Every album I do, I am the quarter-back of the album. No matter what. Every album is 110% Ice Cube. Every track is my vision.

"The music business is basically a pimp relationship. They get all the money for your success and you get peanuts. We have to control the industry. We should make the bulk of the money on our records. There's a lot of people out there who are sick of doing if that way, so we are trying to start up our own businesses to take control of the music. Then we ain't got to answer to anybody. People are starting to realise that America owes us a lot, but it's not going to give us anything that we're not willing to take. All the advancements that we've got in this country, we have initiated. If we want economic growth in our neighbourhoods we have to initiate that, we have to build it. We really have to separate ourselves from this country. Close the doors and say: 'When we get our thing together, we'll open them back up'.

"I think a state is owed to us. The use for the black man and woman in America is over, 1985 it was over. Is a separate state a good idea? Hell yeah, hell yeah.

"What America has got to understand is that if we're going to go down, we're holding onto America and we're going to pull her down too." ■

6

ice-t

One of West Coast rap's best-known and most controversial figures (ironically he was born in New Jersey), Ice-T began releasing records as early as 1983. It was to be eight years before the release of his 'OG: Original Gangster' album propelled him from obscurity into the international mainstream, and since then he has never looked back. While the misogyny, racism and glamorisation of violence in his output are all identifiable (and regrettable) gangsta trademarks, Ice-T deserves his reputation as one of rap's most thought-provoking and versatile stars. He has his own thrash-metal band, Body Count, and has embarked on several parallel careers as a record producer, soundtrack composer, writer and movie actor.

★ ice-t

> " **I**f one person from L.A could break in, then everybody could; it was like a commando mission..."

On being a West Coast rapper...

"It's a very family orientated kind of music, everybody has to be okayed by somebody else to get in. That's what makes it hip. They don't want anybody coming in who doesn't respect rap, who doesn't pay their dues or show respect to people who should get respect. You have to come in and be down with certain people. In the West Coast now, I'm sorry to say, very few people have made the journey to New York to gain respect. They may become big on the West Coast but they won't break that New York iron curtain that I've been working on for years.

"I was lucky because I met all the guys from New York and I got that chance to do a record with Melle Mel. People in New York thought that I must be alright because I'm working with one of the greatest rappers of all time. They let me in.

"New York created rap. It was born in the South Bronx, that's where MCs started rapping to deejays. A lot of kids on the West Coast didn't hear rap until Run DMC came out. New York can give your record the stamp of approval, then everybody else in the USA will also like it."

On the censorship and the PMRC...

The PMRC (Parents Music Resource Centre) opposed and actively attempted to censor much of the violent and profane imagery in rap lyrics. They were virtually instrumental in the 'Parental Advisory: Explicit Lyrics' stickering campaigns of the late '80s – still a common practice. But as Ice-T himself pointed out in the song 'Freedom Of Speech', the move ultimately backfired, the stickers acting more as promotion than the intended deterrent.

"PMRC is just a joke. At the beginning of the 'Power' album, I did all that stuff just for the PMRC. That stuff where the kid gets killed on tape. The PMRC kept saying that I swear on my records and talk about violence, so what am I going to do about it? I said 'Let's kill somebody at the beginning of the album'. I do it just to annoy them; they're not going to stop anything.

"A PMRC sticker just says 'Buy this album, it's bad!' It's like the movies that have ratings, they just help people pick their poison.

"I'm attracting the attention of those people in LA who only understand violence... I'm just here to break rules; anything that can be done, I'm gonna do it.

"My songs are like a movie, they should be an adventure. It's a different style of rap. They aren't about me personally all the time but about things I've seen or heard about. I've got a song called 'The Honeychild' that's about a guy who shot somebody in a club because his boys said: 'Do it'. He does it and he turns around to find that all his friends have gone. Now he's running, he's got no place to hide and nobody wants to know him now. I ain't shot anybody but I know people who have."

On his reputation as a woman-hater...

"Girls say: 'Why do you call girls a bitch on the records?' I say it because that's what I say on the street. I can't help it, I come from a rough neighbourhood and it's not derogatory, it's just how we talk. Everyone can take it how they want to.

"People were coming to me and saying 'Ice, how about making a love song, LL Cool J has done it?' I thought about it and did a song with a more honest approach. The male mentality is that sex comes first and if they like the sex, maybe

they'll get to know the girl. All the nice groups who are after the Coke commercials won't say that. I've got a love song, it's called 'Let's Get Butt Naked And Fuck'."

On the struggle for recognition...

"My first record was similar to what I do now. I had 'Reckless' out [in 1983] but this was my first attempt. This record is me on the street. I was rapping in this beauty parlour to some girls and this dude walked in – Willie Strong – and he said 'Would you like to make a record?' He put me and my buddy in the studio. He had a track with Jimmy Jam and Terry Lewis on it, with some girls singing. He pulled them off and told me to rap – right there! I had never written a song before but raps were in my brain. Those were just straight-up rhymes that I had made. It wasn't contrived in order to be a record, it was what I said on the street. This record coulda been on the 'Iceberg' album. I've gone through a big circle. Between these records I got lost. I was looking for an identity, I wanted to sound like Run DMC, I thought I had to rap about how tough I was. And after I made the Breakin' movies and 'Six In The Morning', that's when my homies said, 'Ice, say that stuff you used to say.'

"It was 'Reckless', on the 'Breakin'' soundtrack. That was a fast record. Then there was a record on Electro Beat called 'Killers' [1983]. This record, 'The Coldest Rap' is two years before Run DMC or LL."

"I didn't get any money for the first record and I signed a contract with them for five years! No records, they just owned me. I think I got maybe a total of $120 in $20-kickouts. I was totally against rap and I was thinking it wasn't gonna work. This is during the time when I was crimin'. I was like a player, the pimp, the women layer, the holy house ruler. If you want to really get into this record, my voice sounds young, but this is the true NWA record. This is a kid in the street stealin', rappin' about his life. I wasn't fantasizin'. I wasn't trying to get no message in that record.

"Okay, record didn't sell, fuck records. I'm gonna keep stealin'. The year the Breakin' movie came out – '84/'85 – this dude in LA, named Alex Jordanoff who was a Russian guy, got hip to hip-hop. He was a grafitti artist and he found this record and realised I was the only LA rapper.

"He said 'Come to my club and rap'. My first performance live I got there and the place was packed. All trendy white kids, and these kids are all here to see Ice T. When I got there they were on this underground tip, I did the song and they knew the words and I went 'Oh shit – this is gonna be my new thing'. So I would do my dirt during the week and then on Friday nights I'd be there and be the star and I got to learn to freestyle. That's where I met Afrika Bambaataa, Afrika Islam [who later became his DJ], Grandmaster Caz, 'cos this guy was from New York and would fly people in to LA. I went up to them and I would say 'You are real rappers, what you think of me?' They were sayin', 'Look, you stay down

with what you doin' 'cos when rap jumps off, you'll be the big shit. If you quit, somebody else'll be the big shit'. But I still didn't think I was gonna make some money doin' it.

"I did the 'Breakin'' soundtrack and the album sold five million records. We got a cheque for $87,000. The Glove, the deejay at the time, gave me $4,000 of the $87,000 because it was his deal. He was the one who got the deal. I was just the featured artist. Then I hooked up with Evil E and Henry G the Spinmasters, They were two guys from New York, they were cool. I went to some of their parties on the East Side, house parties, and I would go there and rap. I had a little rep' from the movies – I was in Breakin', Breakin' II, and a wack movie called Rappin' – terrible movies, you know...

"The kids in Breakdance couldn't really dance, I couldn't really rap. They just wanted something half decent. How were they gonna know good from bad? The movies were a bad scene but you know it kinda kept me employed because I'd cut off my other money and I became the Hollywood rapper. I was the kid in LA who could do the commercials and all that stuff. That's when I went through this thing that I call musical prostitution where you just have to do what you gotta do to get paid.

"Then I did 'Killers' on a label called Electro Beat. I had spikes on and shit. Islam had dressed up like some sort of evil warrior. The record sold a few copies. It wasn't a great record, but it was me still tryin' at it. I thought I should be able to get a record deal. A few more years went by and I hooked up with this buddy of mine who had this label called Techno Hop. I wanted him to make a record with the Spin Masters called 'Yo Stink'. But he said 'You can't sell no records from LA unless they breathed on it – because that was the time of the Egyptian Lover and Wreckin' Cru! I was like, you can sell a record from LA! Let me do it. I had this song called 'Ya Don't Quit' back in the days when 'Inspector Gadget' was out [sings the tune] and I had the music from Bugs Bunny [hums that] and it was time for those hooks. I laid the track down on the 808 [drum machine] and it did good. It was the first real rap record to come off the West Coast other than this buried treasure – 'The Coldest Rap' – that nobody even knows about. That record came out and people said, Ice-T has got a little anger in him, I was screamin' and yellin' and shit. And then I did 'Six In The Morning'.

"That record was a fantasy record which was written to try to capture all the different events that happened to me in my life, but had nothing to do with my life. Nobody could've lived that story and done all the things the guy in 'Six In The Morning' did: 'Up out the window, blue lights, rolled dice, went in jail for seven years, came out'. My attempt is that at one point in the record something happens to you. At one time or another you look in the mirror and say 'Fuck it – blue lights'.

"It's like I added a whole bunch of adventures from kids in the street and I made one person walk the line. That was the first crime rhyme ever written.

"It was wack! So many skeletons. So me and Melle got together. The main objective of that record was for us to get out there. We didn't have a record deal, nobody was gonna sign us. Any record was better than no record. Rap was startin' to happen. Beastie Boys just went platinum and the word was sign rappers, flare went up, Melle was signed to Sugarhill, Grandmaster Caz was signed to Tuff City, Donald D was signed to Vintertainment. I had had records out before and due to the fact that Sire didn't know jack shit about rap, they said 'Sign him'. Fuck it. I lucked up! No skill involved! It had nothin' to do with me bein' good. It was just the right place, right time. I think the fear in knowin' that I didn't get signed 'cos I was dope made me try that much harder 'cos I knew I had snuck in. I wasn't supposed to get no major record deal, and they gave me $40,000, and I went whisperin' 'Oh, please just let me sell 50,000 records so I can make another record'.

"All I really wanted to be able to do was to have my name mentioned along with rappers. When you say Kool Moe Dee and you say Mel, I just wanted my name in there. I never expected for me to be in the top 10 or 20 rappers. Shit! That was beyond my wildest imagination, especially because of being from the West Coast."

On the message in his raps...

There are four themes that run

★ 'Cop Killer' – moi? The Iceman adopts full-on metal pose with his band Body Count

through your raps. The first one is 'Hey educate yourself, because there's no way you can come up and take me over'; the second one deals with LA gang war; the third one is your anti-drug position...

"The fourth one is sex. That's really it. But that's pretty much me. Now sex is the one that most men would just hide. I just try to have fun with it. One time I did a show where I didn't do the nasty rap. It was for Aaron Spelling, who's a big LA producer – he does 'Dynasty' and all that. I'm in this room with all these millionaires and I didn't do no nasty raps. These three 50-year-old white women took me to the coat room and they said, 'Ice-T, what happened to your erotic rhyme? My daughter comes to your club every Friday night and she said you have the most splendid sexual rhyme'. So, I'm standing in the coat room among these mink coats sayin' nasty rhymes to these old women. They're giggling, and they're bugging, but it's the kind of thing that's very taboo. It's kinda like Ice-T can say it to them, but to their boyfriend, 'You don't try it!'. Like Eddie Murphy can talk nasty, but you don't try it. It's gonna turn a lot of women off, but a lot of women trip because it's bold arrogance and it's not to be taken that seriously."

Because of your 'nasty rhymes', people have you marked as sexist?

"If I'm so sexist, why do the women write in about how much they like 'Let's Get Butt Naked And Fuck'. I'm maybe sexist to a hardcore avid feminist. If they would let their hair down and realize that it's just nasty talk... I would have

somebody go against me if I made records about blatant rape.

"Of course I'm against rape, child molestation, stupid shit like that, but two people havin' a good time, enjoyin' themselves – safe, because of that disease! If you can do that, there wouldn't be no war. When two people are gettin' busy there's nothin' better than that. You don't need no dope, no heroin.

"But if you really want to get down to my attitude, the only reason we are put down here on this Earth is to reproduce. If somebody can come up with some other reason for life, please do."

To get back to the gangs and drugs... you're not playing around with that?

"No, no, no, no! You'd know by the tone of the record if I'm serious. I'm definitely serious about the gang shit. That is something that I wish could stop. The gang shit is something that's small but it's big. What feeds the gangs is the same thing that feeds the country, which is why we fightin' and why we feud. I ain't in no gang but four days ago one of my buddies got killed. *Killed.* He was sittin' in a tow truck and they shot him and one of his partners in the head 'til he was dead. This particular guy who shot him is walkin' the streets. Cops ain't gonna do shit. Some of my friends found out who he was. I ain't no gangbanger, but I just can't see him walkin' the streets. He can't just kill my friend like no pig. When he killed him he said, 'Fuck him and fuck all you niggers that know him, you are all punks'. It comes to a point where the rationality clicks off and you think, this guy is still alive! That revenge shit is some awesome shit! Aw, he's dead. Police ain't gonna put anybody away.

"That gang shit is real deep, that's why at the end of 'Color' [from the soundtrack to Colors, LA gangsta flick starring Sean Penn] I said, 'Gangs in LA, our war will end when all wars cease'. Because if you think that gangs will end with the snap of a finger, you might as well go to Northern Ireland and snap your finger or go to Beirut and snap your finger and say quit! It's wrong. It's a war. People are set up. People die. The big difference is between letting him get his butt kicked and gettin' him. It was like Ice, go to Europe, man, because suddenly I got on automatic pilot. If some of my friends got killed, you couldn't talk to me, you know.

"I understand it is real sad, it is real fucked-up. All I can do is try to educate these guys to say 'Hey, let's try to get out, educate the young kids, tell 'em it ain't happening, but it's real fucked up. Once blood has been spilt, it's a war. You got to look at kids who're growin' up and you got to put on a red sweatshirt and somebody says, 'Yo, take off that red sweatshirt because the Blood killed his uncle [Bloods are a LA gang who, as a sign of membership, dress in red. Their major rivals, The Crips, favour blue]. The kid grows up hatin' the colour and he don't even know why. By the time he's 15 he's ready to kill some Blood, because he's bred into this. You go to the funeral and they're all wearing the colours.

"I was involved with the shit so deep. I don't worry about it no more. I'd like to tell them that if they realized who the real enemy was we'd all be on the same side. There's people out there and they want this to go on."

Will you keep doing more raps about gang violence?

"I don't know. I do raps about what's hittin' me at the time. 'Hunted Child' was done to be anti-murder, not anti-gang. 'Killers' was done because one of my buddies got murdered. They put two 45s in his mouth.

"I was in Maui [Hawaii] recently and I was thinkin', 'Wow, this'd be a really nice place to live', but I probably couldn't rap no more 'cos what am I gonna rap about? Palm trees, fish and the deep blue sea? I'd have to start paintin' or something. The shit is just fucked up. I don't know who knows how to end the shit. All I can just do is try."

The same way with drugs?

"You can make a record like 'Self Destruction' [by the Stop The Violence Movement, 1992] and kids will be playin' 'Self Destruction' while they're doin' a drive-by [shooting someone on the street from a car while driving past]. The ones that are ready to do it are gonna do it. The problem is kids have a lot of attitude about it. When I say something to them they say 'Fuck you, what's it got to do with you man, what the fuck are you gonna tell me what I should do!'

Makin' records, it's a trip! They don't want to listen, they might want to kill me. One time I had a gang banger and I said 'Yo, I'm Ice-T'. Well, he said, 'Let me tell you something partner, Ice-T, you a rapper, right? Well, we ain't got no money'. That right there didn't add up with me too good. 'What are you tellin' me?' 'Maybe I should bend you right now 'cos you got money and I don't. All that talkin' is talk and right now I'm hungry'. And I say, 'Okay partner, well I get right back with you'."

Do you ever think about that, somebody coming for you?

"Shit yeah! The jungle creed says the strong must feed on any prey at hand! That's just how the world is. If you weaker than me and I'm hungry you got to go. That's how they gonna do you out there. Some people won't, but that's the law of the jungle."

That sounds like the law you've followed.

"No. I don't follow that law, I'm just aware of that law. I don't follow it or I would be preyin' on people and that's not what I'm about. I'm aware that somebody else bigger than me will take me out if they that kind of person. I ain't living like that. I used to live like that, but I ain't living like that now. I'm trying to live righteously and trying to do the right thing. So I can be Ice.

"Still, you never know what's gonna happen. It's kinda like if you was a doctor in the neighbourhood and you grew up in that neighbourhood and you start out going to school and you get a Mercedes Benz and you want to stay in that neighbourhood, fix your house up, and you forget that everybody around

you is broke; eventually they are comin' to get you because you got money and they don't. It's a cycle.

"My attitude is that people do not live in the ghetto by choice. You live in the ghetto because your parents didn't have enough money to live someplace else. There's no pride in stayin' in the ghetto. Get the fuck outta there. Move into the suburbs. Move next to somebody who don't want you to move next to them. Say hello, I got me some money and I'm out of the fuckin' war zone. Take yourself. Then you spend your money gettin' your homies outta there."

Is that what Rhyme Syndicate – your label and extended posse – is all about?

"Exactly. It ain't about stayin' there. That's one of the mind trips they throw on us. You gotta stay in Brixton, 'cos if you don't stay you ain't down. No, I'm here because I want to get out. I'm gonna bring my mother out, I'm gonna bring my homeboys out, 'cos that is a death pit. That's where they want us all to live.

"But I want to live where I want to live. Someplace nice. And you'll be surprised how, when you try to get out, your homeboys will run that shit on you, like you leavin'! But I got to go! They're sayin' to me: 'Yo Ice, you should come to Brixton', but I'm up here at the Hyatt, why don't you come kick it with me? I spent all my life trying to get the fuck outta the Bronx, come on over to the Marriot. I don't want to go to the Bronx and see that shit."

On acting, prison, and wife Darlene...

"Acting is really something I'd like to get into. Right at the start, when I was crimin' and livin' life day by day, when I was first gettin' down with rap and realizing that there was a career in it, all I wanted to do – my greatest ambition – was to get my name up there with Kool Moe Dee and Melle Mel." And now that it's up there? "Well, I'm happy in what I do now, and now that there's acting there's something else to work on.

"I'm like their number one rapper in there [prison], probably because they are in the best position to know who was really a guy from the streets and who wasn't. That's the reason why no-one in there likes NWA at all, because they are glamorizing violence and jail and to the prisoners, it's obvious that they haven't really experienced it. One guy was more vocal about it, and he said he'd personally see to it that they wouldn't last a week in the yard!

"When I went to the East Jersey State prison in Rahway I hooked up with the Lifers Group [anti-gangsta rap group formed by long term inmates] and did some work with them. Darlene also agreed to do a poster for their campaign too. What I was basically sayin' to the guys in jail was that they didn't have to do crime to make a livin', you can always get money if you work hard for it. It might take longer than if you take the easy way out but it'll come, I ain't lyin'.

"It was like, 'Yeah, I've been heavily involved with the gangs and the crime racket' – I was in there for four years, y'know what I'm sayin'? I got shot twice

and it's not like I'm rapping about something that's a fantasy to me. I've been a hood in the past, but so what? I'm here to talk about the dangers involved, and I'm not out to make it look like somethin' it ain't. I ain't no Vanilla Ice showing the scar where I got stabbed at every press conference. I mean it's like say if I was rapping about Vietnam and sayin' it was great, it'd be obvious I was lyin', and if you had a real Vietnam veteran, you could tell he'd been there 'cos he wouldn't be braggin' about it.

"The way I see it is that Darlene saved my life. She came along when I was kinda at a crossroads in my life – I was trying to decide whether a life in rap or crime was better, and I was kinda losin' the battle 'cos crime was easier and had better rewards.

"Darlene picked me up and convinced me of the talent I had, she told me that crime wasn't the way. She showed me that if I carried on, sooner or later I'd get killed, and all the while before that I'd be fearin' for my life anyway so it had to stop. So she helped me get into rap and got a job and supported me and handled my business... She kept me going. Darlene was the only one to believe in me at that time, and to that end I feel that she's saved my life. Nowadays, it's kinda like at the stage when Darlene doesn't have to do so much as before and now, she kinda like works as my in-house model!"

On the way out of gang warfare...

"The thing is, you've got to

understand why kids get in gangs in the first place. Most of the time kids get in gangs to get known, you know. They want to get that respect. You take away gangbanging, to a lot of these kids it's like taking away their identity.

"See the OGs have got that identity. They've been to jail, they got the tats, they got them war stories. The BGs – the baby gangsters, they want them war stories. They think, 'Are you cutting this game off before I can put some work in?'. They're too young to understand the ramifications.

"But in the areas where the truce started, they ain't letting that shit start back up. Like I just did a video, 'Got A Lot Of Love', over at the Imperial Courts Projects, what they call PJW – Project Watts. The gangs keep a lid on it. And then the girls in the neighbourhood they come in and they say, 'Yep, you done the right thing'. The death toll has dropped extremely. The areas hardest hit by gang violence in the past, they're the ones that are really chill.

"The gangs are saying to themselves, 'Look, if we can sell dope, and if we can run this type of organisation – which is an extremely efficient retaliation machine – we can run businesses. We can do like the mob. Look what the Mafia turned into!"

Some of the major record companies and film studios?

"Yeah, but the media have really shown how they don't give a fuck. They're still only televising the gang deaths. They don't show the kids hugging, the Crips and the Bloods embracing. They don't show that. They show the cops on the perimeter, waiting on trouble."

On hip-hop as an information service...

"The first key to this whole shit is hip-hop. When rap stays in Harlem, nobody gives a fuck. But when white kids start listening to my opinions, when they walk home to moms and say, 'I like Ice-T, Ice's got a point', and mom says, 'Ice-T ain't got no point – Ice-T is black. Then they say: 'I like Too Short too' – 'No, but no no no! Those black guys'll take your money'. And the white kid says 'Fuck that!' He knows that's why we're in this whole situation.

"Homes are being invaded with hip-hop theories and hip-hop flavours. White kids are being injected with black rage and anger. People like KRS-One, Public Enemy, Cube, are stimulating kids to question authority. And mom says, 'My home has been invaded by these new ideas. How did it get in here?' It comes in through the Walkman. These homes are being invaded by us. And they know it. They know we're in their homes.

"Rap was the most information-giving music ever created. Hip-hop injected information back into the people. And Public Enemy came in and put the black into it, and I went into it and I showed people this is what crime is. I showed them this is the brainwave of the gangbanger, this is the brainwave of the cop killer. It's not because of the movie Spike Lee made. It's not these books. The reason he's made that movie, the reason people are reading these books, is hip-hop...

"The album cover says it all," he says, rooting excitedly in his briefcase for the sleeve to 'Home Invasion' [his fifth LP, issued in '93]. The case is full of DAT master tapes. A porn mag falls out. Finally he locates the piece of paper. The picture shows a white teenager strapped to a Walkman. Public Enemy and Ice Cube tapes litter the floor, and streaming out of the kid's head are images of sex and violence.

"He's got the books, too" points out Ice. "There's Malcolm X, Iceberg Slim, Donald Goines. He's got his Fishbone T-shirt... See it started off slow, he was into Fishbone, and now he's got the black pendants on. His eyes are closed. People say, 'Well, why isn't that a black kid?' And I'm saying, 'Because that isn't the problem'. The black kid is listening to it, that's nothing. Right there, this scene here, this is the invasion. If ten black guys listen to the tape, and two white guys, the problem would be the white guys – when they went home and started talking that 'Cop-Killer' shit! You want to know why they went after 2 Live Crew? It's a racial thing. It has nothing to do with them being dirty, it has to do with them doing shows in Miami where there's 20,000 white girls screaming: 'Me so horny'. The system spent a long time trying to make white kids hate black kids on face value. Hip-hop came in and said, 'Wait a minute, you ain't got no reason to hate us'.

"And it's breaking down this whole divide and conquer shit, because the key to keeping people divided is to keep information from them. I'm very cynical as far as free speech goes. If you look at the 'Pusher Man' video – I wrote and directed that video and I predicted that one day rap would be illegal and you would have to sell it out of the trunk of your car like dope.

"And it's going down like that. Luke's [Campbell, founder of 2 Live Crew] tapes have been sold out of the trunk. Like a drug! The Body Count shit is out on the street right now. It is illegal to have it and sell it.

"My favourite line was something Chuck [D] wrote: 'I don't rhyme for the sake of riddling'. He was saying, 'Yo, I got a reason to do this shit'. Say something serious, man. Look at my albums. This is what I learnt, this is what I felt. It's like I'm shooting my wad every year. Blam blam blam."

On hard work and 'Cop Killer'...

Ice-T knew he had really made the big time when the 'Cop Killer' controversy erupted. Not a rap record, but a track on the eponymous debut LP of his spin-off hardcore band Body Count, it was condemned as dangerous and inflammatory by everyone from the police to (then) US president George Bush. At one point it was even revealed that Ice was listed as number two on the FBI national threat list. Despite agreeing to remove (and effectively censor) the song from the LP, the issue ultimately ended with Ice being released from his contract with Time-Warner.

"I'm a very loyal person," says Ice-T, "and I bill myself on my integrity. If I say I'm gonna do something I'm gonna do it. I've got my ill side to me too – I'm into Jason and Freddie Krueger, I can watch that shit all night but I'm pretty much somebody who's willing to try things. I'm a tryer. I'm not somebody who's into saying 'I can't do it'. I guess that's what they'll write on my tombstone – HE TRIED.

"'Home Invasion' was like having a baby, it took nine months to get it out," he laughs. "Warners were very cool about it. They cut me a release date, gave me all my tapes back, it was cool.

"But then the press writes up 'Ice-T is dropped!' Every chance they can the mainstream press tries to make me look weak. Like when we pulled 'Cop Killer' it was our decision. We pulled it, they said 'Ice-T Gives In To Dan Quayle'. Fuck Dan Quayle! I don't give a fuck about him. Fuck the police! I just did it because I got tired of seeing myself on the news. I thought that the cops were using me to cover up what they were doing. It was a way of saying, 'You think we did it for money? Fuck that record. The record's no longer on Warner Brothers so leave that alone and I'll give the fucking record away.' So it was like a chess game that was going on at that time.

"Y'know I really don't even have anything to say about 'Cop Killer' any more because none of my fans got mad at it anyway. It's like I'm spending a lot of time trying to convince people who don't listen to my music what it's about. Why even waste time? There's a point where it gets stupid. I didn't get a gang of people who buy Ice-T records mad at me, it was a group of people who don't even know who the fuck I am, who was calling this rock album a rap album. Why even entertain them with explanations about it? Fuck them. Everybody who's bought the record knows what it's about. For now, let's everybody hear what censorship is really like."

On the LA riots and their aftermath...

"LA is kinda laidback. The gang truce has about one third of the gang members at peace. That's a lot. They've been gangbanging out there for about 20 years so I don't expect to see it end in one year. We've got a third this year and maybe by this time next year we'll have half the people at truce and move on. I'm looking at a three-year plan to turn this place into peace. You gotta have hope because I've never seen one gang member at truce so when I'm looking at 30,000 kids hugging, there's a lotta hope there. So I'm just trying to perpetuate it.

"The problem is that the Government has this thing that they play called Truth or Consequences. Meaning, if we commit a crime, they issue a consequence. My question to these people is if they commit a crime, how do we issue consequences? Vote? I don't think so.

"What you saw in LA, regardless of how unfocussed, wrong or harmful that might have been, it was a consequence.

And if that hadn't happened there'd have never been another trial. Sometimes the people do have to rise up and demonstrate – that was a very radical demonstration, but that's what it was really, a way of saying 'Look man, you've gotta give us some justice or somebody's gonna get hurt'.

"I've made a statement saying that in a way it was a great thing and people say that 'How can you make that comment, you didn't get something burned down...' But what I meant was it was great just to see the people stand up. I just hope it doesn't happen again because I think that the next time people are going to get really hurt...

"Race war is what I see coming if people don't get their head in check. What I hope to do with that record is let people see how confused they are. Like when I say 'Orientals are black', I wanna make you see how confused you are so you don't even know who to fight. Right now the way they got everybody hating each other you'd probably go out and just kill some boy who's a different colour than you just outta ignorance. I'm saying there's gonna be a lotta white kids rollin' with the Africans, there's gonna be a lot of blacks that are on the other side, so it's gonna be real fucked up. So let's try to avoid this at all cost. You know when they asked me about free speech I told them, same with the riots and that's what's gonna happen next.

"I definitely believe in the unity of oppression. "I'm promoting it from 'Mama's Gotta Die Tonight' [from 'Body Count'] to just trying to check and figure out that all the people being oppressed are on the same side and have the same enemy. So let's go get them, don't let them trick us into getting each other."

On family life...

"I'm not going to tell you that I would sit my son down in front of a porno movie or anything, but if I came home and discovered him watching one I wouldn't assume it's the first one he's ever seen. Then it would probably be a good time to talk to him about sex and find out just how much about this stuff he does understand. Although the porno movie isn't love, it is sex and, though I wouldn't be mad at him for watching it, I don't know if I would tell him it was alright for him to watch them around me.

"I think there has to be a level of respect between the son and the father. My father would always curse me but I would never curse him back. I don't think it's healthy to be too level with your children but as for censoring them from real life, I'm not with that bullshit. The quicker they see the shit, the better!

"People tell me if I put him in a private school he's going to end up being a nerd and that's impossible – just look who his dad is! He'll pick up all the street shit in the world at home from his uncles, all ex-cons. I think most Mafia bosses would send their sons to private school."

On juggling his different careers...

"Right now I'm juggling all my careers about. I am concerned though about all of

★ **OG: Original Gangster – the coldest rapper cuts the ice**

them and I wouldn't want to See Body Count fall off because of my Ice-T career or the acting. If anything I'll continue my music career because that's what means the most to me. Acting is pretending to be someone else while my rap career is me. It's what I've always wanted to do and it's what I'm always going to do."

Ice-T rapping all the way to the pension shop?

"I never thought you could do this at 50 years old, but now I think you can," he proudly proclaims. "The audience will grow up with me. You see, the kids who like me now were 15 when they started liking me and now they're 24. I grew up with them so why wouldn't they still want to listen to me? The same people who grew up listening to the Rolling Stones now listen to Mick Jagger.

"Guru's 'Jazzmatazz' is very adult rap and I don't see any reason why there has to be an age limit to performing rap; there's no age limit in rock. For fuck's sake look at Kiss!

"The way you attract the younger fans is by always featuring the new kids on your albums. That is what has really kept Dr Dre at the rap forefront, because he has brought in Snoop and the whole of the Dogg Pound...

"Quincy Jones said the truest thing ever to me when he said, 'Ice, no matter what you do something new will come out each year and never turn on that. Try and absorb it into your music or you'll turn into your own enemy. You'll start to sound like all those people who harp on about the good ol' days.' I do try and keep

with the new stuff, but I'll always maintain who I am."

On fame and the pursuit of happiness...

"Yeah, I'm happy, but I still feel a lot of anger and pain for the problems that other people have still got. People say, 'Ice-T's got paid, he doesn't care any more'. That's just bullshit.

"It's like saying, if I had AIDS then was cured I wouldn't care about people who've got AIDS. It's shit. Yes, I got out of the ghetto and now I know how nice it is not to be in the ghetto. Now I'm that much more mad about the conditions my friends have to live in.

"I'd be a liar if I said I wasn't happy. I think I'm one of the only people I know who can honestly say they've done everything they ever wanted to do. I wanted to be a rapper. I did it. I used to watch TV and want to play rock 'n' roll. I used to want to be able to get up on stage and go wild and I did that. Everyone watches TV and I thought, wouldn't it be nice to actually be on TV. I did that. Cover of a magazine. Done it. Brand new car. Got it. Bought a house, had a son, got a beautiful girl.

"Now I've done all that, lived that life, I want to show other people what it's like to do those things. It's kind of like going to an amusement park on your own, it's no fun unless you can take a friend along for the ride. That's real fun and that's what being on these tours is like.

"These guys in Body Count have never been out of the 'hood before. They're like Ice-T ten years ago. They're so excited going abroad, they've all gone out and bought their first video cameras to capture everything they see. I'm like a kid all over again and it's fun. I'm just going to see how many times I can fuck this industry up...!

"I can't even begin to imagine what it would be like to operate in this industry and be fucked up on drugs. If you want that flash car, that platinum album and a million dollars you can't afford to fuck around. If success was easy to come by, everyone would be living the good life.

"I never get caught up in any showbusiness bullshit. You must have all heard about new crews going out and smashing up their hotels on their first tour and getting fucked up every night at parties with groupies and all the rest. You'd be amazed at the way my crew moves. We check into a hotel, play a show and then we're out of there and on our way to another town. No messing, no fussing and no fucking up. We've all got families and kids to support, so there's no way we can afford to fuck around with our jobs, our incomes.

"In this business you have one chance and if you blow that, there's no guarantee you'll ever get another shot at success. I'm a rapper who's been around for six albums and never once had to make a comeback. Comeback? I never ever want to make a comeback!

"A lot of these so-called gangsters and hardcore rappers build up images of what they claim to be for everyone to see. Now I personally don't feel I need to build up any image of myself, I don't need to prove how tough I am or how hard I am. I'm not saying everything you hear me saying on record is true or anything because a lot of it is just dramatic bullshit. Do you really think Scarface murders 15 people in one song alone? But to me, what you say on wax doesn't have to correspond with how you act when you're just around normal people. The guys who go around all the time talking tough and acting like they're gangsters – they're fake.

"I grew up around very hardcore individuals. I myself could be considered a very hardcore individual, considering some of the things I have done in my life against other people, but for me to act hard against you would just be plain stupid. I don't have a reason to fear you and I don't have a reason to make you fear me. We're in a perfectly normal situation and I'm not out to impress upon you how 'real' I am or how 'street' I am. I drink milk, I play Nintendo, you saw me reading the Sega magazine on the tour bus and I don't have a problem with people seeing that side of me. Having said all that though, I wouldn't advise you to fuck around with me...

"Every year I feel like I have to prove something, even if it's just to prove to myself that I can make a better record than last time. I think the main reason I've never been forced to make a comeback is because I've never really been that large. In America I'm only now getting my first platinum album, which is for 'Power' [his second LP from 1988]. I'd always sell between 700,000 and

900,000 copies, but I'd never have a platinum record. LL Cool J would sell two million records and then Run DMC would sell three million records, but I'd always just keep dipping under the million mark. I guess Kris (KRS-One) has always been closer to me in terms of consistent sales than anyone else, but then that's worked in our favour. We've both always had a solid fan base and that's important if you aim to stick around in this industry.

"I'm not saying it's easy to be in my position – it's not. In fact, it's getting more stressful the bigger I become. I had no idea 'Home Invasion' would sell so well [it's his biggest selling album in Europe] but in the States it never sold as well as 'OG'. That's cool, though. I'm not worried because Ice-T albums sell over long periods of time. I don't see it as a sign that I've fallen off because the fans will tell you in no uncertain terms if you've fallen off."

On the future and his hip-hop identity...

"The new album which I'm working on now ['Return Of The Real'] is the best album I've ever done. 'Home Invasion' was written during the whole 'Cop Killer' fiasco and I was a very angry man... It showed when you listened to the album. It's a very self-centred album but my new album will sound a lot more focussed. The beats are better, the concepts are better and the stories I tell are better. It is going to be a real Ice-T album. If there's things missing from 'Home Invasion' then they'll be there.

"It's hard for me to make an album

that is 100% Ice-T because there's so much going on around me. When I'm in the studio I have to wear blinders so I can just get on with my work and forget about everybody else in hip-hop. I'll be in the studio and Cypress Hill will be blowing up, Lords Of The Underground will be the mad flavour or Redman will be it, but I have to keep concentrating on who and what Ice-T is. I can't make a Das-EFX record, I have to be me and you'll maybe see slight influences from another group in my records but you'll never see total change.

"Fame is something that you need to acquire real gradually. It's something which you've got to learn to really respect otherwise it'll take you out. Fame is also something which nearly always arrives before the money. You get famous and then you can't work because you don't want to be on TV and work at the same time.

"I'll never forget when I first started. One time I was riding the bus and these kids saw me and they were straight over asking what I was doing on the bus. I told them my car was broke and they just couldn't believe it. They couldn't believe the rapper might only have one car – a broken one! They just wouldn't leave it alone either, so I lied and told them I was shooting a video and if they waved they'd be in the video. They were happy then because they really didn't want to believe that Ice-T might not be as big as they thought. I lied to them but, in a way, I think it was better to lie than to burst those little kids' bubble.

"Being famous is hard sometimes because you've got to be aware that when people like you they like you, but when they turn against you they can be your worst enemy...

"What I've tried to do is never to be in a position I don't want to be in. When I feel like being around fans I'm happy to sign autographs and talk with them, but when I'm not in the mood I just try and disappear...then there's no way you can get mad with me. Sometimes it's just a matter of catching someone at exactly the right time, otherwise you're going to be disappointed.

"I think fame, especially too much of it, is probably my ultimate fear. When there comes a time that I just can't walk down the street because I'm too famous. that's when everything's got too far out of hand. I've always had a special kind of fame because I've always known that it's been the rap kids who like me.

"Now, through Body Count and through my film career [Ice's film credits already include 'New Jack City', 'Trespass', 'Surviving The Game' and 'Tank Girl'] people from all walks of life know who Ice-T is and that's real scary. I couldn't imagine being Eddie Murphy or Michael Jackson... People always laugh at me because I'm more worried about fame than death, but death is nothing to fear. Once you die there's no more cable bill, no more phone bill, no more bills whatsoever! The only pain is the pain you leave in the people you leave behind... Where's the big deal?

"I've provided for my family and I've got life insurance, so I know they'll all be alright if I die, but then I think my son and my daughter need a father figure, and that gives me every reason to want to live. I've always been like a father-type figure so I wouldn't say it's really changed me at all.

"Kids are just here to make you realise what life is all about. You are never going to achieve something which would even come close to creating a kid. Records, TV shows... bullshit! You make a life, now *that's* a responsibility. Fuck... that's all we're on Earth to do." ■

7

jazzy jeff

& the fresh prince

DJ Jazzy Jeff and The Fresh Prince have become a far more durable act than their 'novelty' late '80s hits, 'Girls Ain't Nothing But Trouble' and 'Parents Just Don't Understand', suggested. The first rap act to be nominated for a Grammy award (for 'Parents...'), the duo boycotted the awards ceremony because it was due to be censored before being broadcast on TV. Despite several such gestures, however, the group have often been criticised as not 'hard' enough – an impression given weight by the Prince's reincarnation as a TV star in 'The Fresh Prince Of Bel-Air', and by the release of further highly-commercial recordings such as 'Summertime' (another Grammy winner) and the UK chart-topping single 'Boom! Shake The Room'.

★jazzy jeff & the fresh prince

"**B**asically," says Jeff, "we're snubbed because we've sold over three million albums, not because we've turned into a pop group... We're certainly not a pop group."

The musical mastermind behind this Philadelphia-raised duo – both born in 1968 – Jeff [Townes] started deejaying at the tender age of ten, assuming control of the decks at parties when his elders took a toilet break. It was at another house party, then in his late teens, that Jeff hooked up with the Fresh Prince and they pursued a recording contract. Their progress was greatly enhanced when Jeff landed the coveted Battle Of The Deejays trophy at the 1986 New Music seminar in New York.

"The way I see it is that there's room for everybody and every style. We're not doing anything different now than from when we first started out [with the acclaimed 'Rock The House' LP in '87]. The direction we take is ours and up to us – we just became a little more successful than some others... No, a *lot* more successful.

"The media is very racist and controlled by a white majority. Basically, we as black people have to take what's ours 'coz nothing's going to be given to us for free. It was about time that a rap act appeared on the David Letterman Show. The audience was obviously not used to what they saw when we went on, but they had to get wise real quick. They enjoyed it once they worked out what was going on.

"America isn't synonymous with white. It's a multi-cultural land and we're going to tread on all that land that we're not supposed to walk." Even after winning the accolade of Best Rap Performers at the prestigious Grammy Awards, Jazzy Jeff & Fresh Prince decided to prompt their rap buddies such as Salt-N-Pepa, LL Cool J, Kid-N-Play and Slick Rick into boycotting the awards ceremony. Why?

"They didn't want to acknowledge rap music for what it really is," answers Jeff.

"There ain't no one who can tell me that rap music isn't one of the top five money making and most popular music mediums of 1988/89.

"They were making out they didn't have enough time to show all the rap nominees because they only had enough time to televise 19 categories, five of which were Country & Western.

"They wanted us to settle for being the token rap group and go on and give a 30-second message. We shouldn't stand for it. There needs to be categories at the Grammies for Best Rap Performer, Best Rap Single, Best Rap Newcomers, Best Video and all that, and if it doesn't look like they've recognized the need for that this year, we'll boycott it again, even if we win.

"Unfortunately Kool Moe Dee and JJ Fadd didn't want to take part in the boycott and appeared on the show so we don't really know if we got our point across."

"We have our views, but we don't believe in forcing them down people's throats," offers the Fresh Prince. "I'm not dissing groups like PE or NWA when I say this but, as I see it, you don't pay money to go to a concert and be yelled and screamed at – it's okay if you know the approach that these guys take, but if you wanna have a good time come and see us."

On the secret of their success...

Jeff: "Honestly, we can't put our finger on our success. To me it's bein' in the right place at the right time. I'd love

to take the credit and say it's because we're this and we're that but... it's not the case. 'Parents Just Don't Understand' was the right record at the right time, played for the right people. The only thing you can try and do is plan your luck – I mean, a lot of the time we try and work out what might work ten years from now, or what might work next year. Sometimes you're right and sometimes you're not!

"We have to give credit where credit is due – if it wasn't for Run DMC, Jazzy Jeff & the Fresh Prince wouldn't be where we are today, and if it wasn't for us, maybe Hammer wouldn't be where he is. Hammer took rap music and surpassed almost every other music – he totally legitimised rap music. You can't say that rap music is small business anymore."

On 'The Fresh Prince Of Bel-Air'...

The Fresh Prince's enormous success in this prime time sit-com has helped paved the way for other rappers to turn their attentions to mainstream acting roles, such as Queen Latifah in 'Living Single' and LL Cool J in 'In The House'. Meanwhile Will has taken on increasingly dramatic film roles in the likes of 'Six Degrees Of Separation' and 'Bad Boys'.

"The show's doin' really well. I was on about nine episodes last year and I'm a recurring character this year. It's a lotta fun to do, and one thing we really like about it is, what you see is exactly how we are. People say, 'You guys do so well', but it's not like we're acting. We're just taking our real-life situations – the way we talk, the way we act – and puttin' it on screen. People can relate to it because they say 'Well man, these guys are real'.

"The show also likes to tackle situations that other shows won't tackle. They did an episode on black-on-black prejudice and one of the things we're looking to tackle is the gang problem. We wanna talk about what happens before you get to that situation. People are always talkin' about what happens after you're in the situation, while we wanna talk about what gets you there. There's a lot of social things you can have fun with, and also prove a point."

Jeff: "I wanted to remain just doing the music, but eventually Will [Smith, aka the Fresh Prince] twisted my arm to do some guest roles. I did it for the fun! I mean, it's cool to make money, but if you don't enjoy doin' what you wanna do then it's not worth it!"

On 'Summertime'...

"Y'know, just waxing down your car, goin' crusin', seein' all you friends, goin' to the hang-out spot – that's what it's about" explains Jeff. "As the song came about we realised 'Summertime' was something everybody could relate to – you'll sit and say, 'Well, how did I spend my Summertime in England?' You didn't do what we did, but you did your own thing.

"We'd 'finished' the album ['Homebase'] about five times and kept saying, 'Let's do one more track...' and the record company said 'let's get Hula

and Fingers to do one or two tracks as a bonus'. Everyone was open-minded about it and 'Summertime' was perfect!

"When I heard the song, there was nothing I could do to it because everything was there. The only thing I did was the remix – the icing on the icing on top of the cake!

"This album's a shocker 'cos it's a 180-degree turn from everything that Jazzy Jeff and the Fresh Prince ever did. I think we've already stated the shock with 'Summertime' because few people believe it's Jazzy Jeff and the Fresh Prince. It's just getting older – Will is four years older than he was on 'Parents Just Don't Understand' – and I've grown a lot as a producer, become a lot more musical, and all this showed

"This album's a lot more dance-orientated, the grooves are very light, the raps are very short and it's definitely gonna be a surprise to everyone who hears it."

On not being 'hard' enough...

"It doesn't really bother me," shrugs Jeff. "Right now, rap is so broad and, to me, rap is not one music – it's a lyrical form over any music. You can look at what Public Enemy do as almost like BB King – rappin' about social and conscious things, it's almost like the blues. Then you have Jazzy Jeff and The Fresh Prince who do fun-loving things that make you feel good like the Beach Boys. Then you have a group like 2 Live Crew who could actually be like an Old Blowfly or Richard Pryor.

"You can't categorise rap because there are so many different types. There's a side in me that's socially conscious that draws me to Public Enemy, but I also like Sting! There's many people inside me that make up the whole.

"You always think that, that thing about 'why us?' But things have been happening so quickly for the both of us that we're not in the position to have the opportunity to stop and think about what's been happening. Before we had the chance to stop and say 'Damn!', it had become a global thing."

"You never truly feel you deserve what you have, you just feel blessed," adds the Fresh Prince. "Right now I've got to a point with my television career where I can do what I want. The film career is something different, I'm just starting out there. But with Jazzy Jeff, we've always been able to do exactly what we want to do.

"For us, it's all about timing. In rap there's such a high volume of records that the urge is to put out the next record as quickly as possible. You have to make the turnaround time from album to album very quick indeed. It stems from the record companies and their initial reaction to rap. At first they wouldn't go near it, in the early days, because they thought it wasn't going to last. Then when they realised that it was, they signed up everybody, which was, y'know, negative to the music, because rap wasn't so specific, there was too much coming out at once.

"I think rap will always be there in some shape or form because it's a poetry. It's just going to keep changing shape. It's always been around, except now it's called rap. When The Last Poets ['60s forerunners of rap who pioneered the 'talking jazz' movement] were doing it, when Shakespeare was doing it, it was called something different. Romeo & Juliet, it's a rap!"

"I think rap will eventually become pop music," says Jazzy Jeff. "All pop will have a hip-hop base. People are already using breaks from old hip-hop records to make new pop records. For a while a break was James Brown, y'know. Now it could be an old Public Enemy sample."

"That's the thing about Run DMC," adds the Prince. "They made rap international."

Is rap a multi-cultural thing then, that everybody's trying to pigeonhole?

"Completely. And one day soon people are gonna realise that." ∎

8

krs-one

Releasing records for years under the
Boogie Down Productions label, KRS-One
(it stands for 'Knowledge Reigns
Supreme Over Almost Everyone') is now
recognised as a hip-hop pioneer, skilled
producer and astute social commentator
in his own right. BDP's first album,
'Criminal Minded', was arguably the
first record to reflect and encourage the
gangsta lifestyle. But after the murder
of the group's Scott La Rock in 1987,
KRS-One shifted the emphasis from
aggression to a message of peace,
tolerance and 'edutainment'. A tireless
campaigner whose output includes books
and lecture tours as well as rap records,
KRS-One continues to speak for his
community with a voice whose wisdom
and clarity few young artists can match.

★ krs-one

"**A**merica was founded by criminals, it was built by criminals, and it has had criminal acts throughout its history — which some people call 'a country growing up'. The government, Congress and so on, are criminal minded. They control the media, but we're not allowed to control anything except what we work for. That's criminal minded."

On the 'Criminal Minded' album...

Born Lawrence Kris Parker in 1966, KRS-One met his late DJ Scott La Rock at a homeless people's shelter in the Bronx — La Rock was a counsellor, KRS his client. Produced in conjunction with the equally influential Ultramagnetic MCs, 'Criminal Minded' (1987) depicted the duo brandishing firearms on its sleeve.

"A government is a government for the people by the people, but it's got to the point in 1988 where our government does just what it wants to, and the public has to suffer the consequences regardless.

"The public should unite against the government; then you would notice the country change dramatically. But for me to think like that, I'm thinking criminal minded, I'm thinking like a criminal. That's treason here in in America!

"I'm not pointing the finger at any particular president or government, to say that they're wrong for being criminal minded. I am saying that in some way we should educate the people on how to be criminal minded. It's like, in order to survive in a criminal minded society you have to think criminal minded, you have to be taught criminal education. But people are not being taught that, and as a result you find people who just can't cope in today's society."

On 'By All Means Necessary' and the nature of peace...

Released the following year minus La Rock — who was murdered while sitting in a car in the South Bronx — the LP's grainy black and white sleeve featured a semi-automatic weapon. This time, however, there was a method to the madness.

"I contradicted myself on purpose. I put a gun on the cover, mean face, black kid holding a gun, looking out of a window, but in the music there's songs like 'Stop the Violence'. I even have a poem on the album – I mean, how soft can you possibly get? But yet, in the face of hardcore America I'm classed as one of the most hardcore artists out here.

"The poster represents Malcolm X exercising his constitutional right to bear arms whenever he felt his life was in danger. I used that picture for several reasons. One was a philosophical reason, meaning that it's time for at least one recording artist to bear some sort of educational arms, because the life of hip-hop music is in danger.

"The second was because of the fact that I went to a new, major label, and because Scott La Rock passed away. The audience are the first to say that you've gone soft. You know: he's gone to a new label, he's commercialised on RCA, his partner died so now he's really soft. The media wanted me to come out with a soft, wishy-washy image, so what I did was I dared them. I came back on the cover with the same hardcore, strong image, daring the media and also telling the public that nothing changes in our campaign.

"The third reason was that, in fighting for world peace we must throw away the stereotype that peace is a flower. That's the wishy-washy stereotype image, and it's not the image we're aiming at. We're fighting now for political awareness, public awareness and world peace. In order to bring this about we have to be stronger than war. Peace has to be stronger than war. In other words, if war is carrying a .22, peace has to carry a magnum, peace has to carry an Uzi.

Peace has to constantly overcome war in order to win in its own name.

"It's impossible for you to say that you're all for peace and then carry a flower in the midst of people with nuclear arms. You don't get anywhere and ultimately a statement that doesn't get anywhere, doesn't do anybody any good.

"The new hardcore image is of the intelligent B-boy who can speak on issues like stopping the violence in hip-hop, or illegal business controlling America, and at the same time listen to tracks like 'Jimmy', 'Ya slippin'', 'My Philosophy' and 'I'm Still #1'. We're staying in this mainstream of rap music, but at the same time we're teaching the new hardcore. So I wouldn't say that the cover [of 'By All Means Necessary'] is promoting any sort of violence. The reality of the situation is that music does not promote violence, but the artist has the opportunity to either promote violence or do away with it.

"I would say that my album cover is violent to the people I'm talking about, but it's not violent to the people I'm talking to. I'm talking about the government, about stereotypes in the music industry. To these people I am violent, and it's because I'm speaking the truth about them…

"New York is a hardcore city, so it's no problem for the album to be played here, but outside of New York City they can't even relate to the music. It's like they're not even ready for it; they're still with LL and Run DMC. Their interpretation of hardcore is yelling over a hard beat. I don't do much yelling, I just put emphasis on what I'm saying.

"So you have this situation where people are saying they can't play the album, yet in that same town I'm sold out. These people don't want to play the album because they're scared to take a risk and they're scared of change; they're scared to educate the people for fear of what might become of their own jobs.

"Even in New York the DJs won't play 'Illegal Business', because it's scary, it's very, very scary. Put yourself in the position of a radio DJ. You have a boss who, when you say 'rap' to him, he thinks it means Run DMC and LL Cool J. Now, you're going to play something on prime-time radio, or on any of their major radio stations, which says 'illegal business controls America, cocaine business controls America', they get scared. All of a sudden your phones light up. The kids want to hear that record again every single day. So, rather than start the trend of having a hit record like 'Illegal Business' being played over and over again, they just don't play it. But between myself and Public Enemy, we'll change that within about a year. Give it about a year and they'll be able to play stuff like 'Illegal Business'."

On the threat of drugs and racism...

"The kids love the music. Everybody in the public loves the music. As for the government, I don't know, maybe they've staked me out already. But the kids know exactly what time it is with that.

It's so blatant, so open, about what's going on with this illegal business. But it's really no big deal, you know?

"I made the record because no-one else would talk about the situation. Crack dealers, drug dealers selling anything, and there's police officers standing within a hundred yards of them, you know what I mean? It's just a way of life here. No-one really downs it, no-one says it's bad. But it's wrong for the media to try and cover it up.

"Uniting the black race is a step towards the ultimate goal of uniting all the races. You can't unite any race with another race until they are united in themselves. Personally, I don't think even the white race is united. They need someone to speak out for them. The only race I can think of who have found some sort of unity through their culture is the oriental race of people. They have some sort of order and respect among themselves. But the white race is totally broken apart through money and greed and selfishness, and the black race is totally broken apart through money and greed and envy and jealousy. It's time for someone to speak out for the white race, to unite the white race, and for someone to unite the black race, and ultimately for the world to be united.

"Every race has its negative people, every race has its positive people. It's time for the positive people to weed out the negative and give them one decision: to move forward for peace and justice or be destroyed. That'll be the only way to gain some sort of justice, some sort of peace around this world.

On the 'Ghetto Music: The Blueprint Of Hip Hop' album...

An album a year was now the norm for BDP, with KRS's messages becoming increasingly conscious. He was instrumental in expanding rap's public image by setting out on lecture tours of prominent American universities (including Yale and Havard), and was also writing columns for the New York Times.

"'Who Protects Us From You?' is directed towards the Police Department, or any authority figure who has the power to arrest. It's just basically: 'Who are you protecting, the rich, the poor, who?' I live in a rich community now, and I see that the police in this community are more prone to help you, no matter what your colour is. In the ghetto community, they're looking for you to do something wrong. So that record was written to ask them: 'Who are you protecting? You're put here to protect us, but who will protect us from you?' If they shoot a black kid in the ghetto, it doesn't normally make news. What makes news is if a black kid shoots a cop, white or black. What I'm saying is there's no law that protects the poor from the authorities.

"Ghetto music is not only the blueprint of hip-hop, it's the blueprint of all music, every piece of music from country, rock, jazz... everything was created first in the ghetto and then commercialised on. Thus it's happening with rap. Rap was created in the ghetto and now it's becoming more and more commercial, so we seek to bring things down to their roots in 'Ghetto Music'. We glorify the underground artist and take a little of the credit away from the more commercialised artist.

"'World Peace' speaks for itself. If you want world peace, take it. It's a different approach to the common world peace attitude of protesting, flower children and so on. This is the more radical concept of world peace, it's more the concept of Armageddon. If you want world peace, take it, 'cos a lot of our leaders fake it.

"'World Peace' is a message to everyone, whoever buys the album. World peace is not a thing to wait for, you have to take it physically, mentally and verbally, in other words replacing lies and stereotypes of races, of both the white race and black race. There are some ridiculous stereotypes of white race and some ridiculous stereotypes of black race that need to be erased so that all people of all races can get the clear picture. Then we'll be on the road to world peace, but as long as we are blind to this we'll have the concept of looking at each other and saying 'Well, who are you? I'm better than you'. If you want world peace, take it on all levels.

On the HEAL compilation album, 'Civilisation Versus Technology'...

After inaugurating the Stop The Violence Movement – which raised 600,000 dollars for the National Urban League in 1991 – KRS poured his energies into this human awareness project, notably enlisting the services of REM vocalist Michael Stipe.

"Civilisation versus technology, that's the war that we're fighting right now. No-one's civilised, everyone's technological, and we're losing out because of it. We're dying as a civilisation and rising fast as a technological society. Soon we'll all be robots.

"When civilisation leads technology, you have a good school system, you have doctors, medicine, tools to build things with. When civilisation is ruling technology, you have these things like boats and so on, things to help your society along. But when technology leads civilisation, you have a corrupt government, a corrupt school system, the atomic bomb, all forms of weapons, things that are used to destroy your society. What's happening is that technology is leading because we never really were civilised.

"The Romans were one of the first technological societies. They were the most significant because they invaded Africa and destroyed large parts of civilised Africa, Asia, all parts of the East. They just went through and destroyed in the name of Great Rome and Greece and Persia and these people.

"They were more technological, in other words they had bigger spears, and bows and arrows with poison tips and all kinds of craziness. They had faster boats, also. The Africans didn't have that, they had great libraries, and politics, government, lawyers and doctors and so on. That's a civilisation. All that was destroyed by technology, and we have

never regained it.

"So this is the basis behind the HEAL book and also the album itself, 'Civilisation Versus Technology'. We need to become more civilised. In the book I give a couple of definitions to both words. Like one, technology is the science of mechanical and industrial arts, according to various dictionaries, and civilisation is an advanced stage in social development, 'social' being the interaction between human beings towards one another. So, just because we cannot get along simply implies that we are uncivilised. The minute we can get along with one another in an advanced social way, we become civilised, we become a civilisation.

"But there is a master plan to have the mass of civilised people uncivilised. Within their uncivilisation they ultimately walk around blind, and they don't get to see the technological society that's destroying all of them. It's not a white thing, it's not a black thing, it's not an Asian or an Indian thing, it's a human thing, and we're totally missing the point if we're looking at black and white. Which isn't to say that if you're black you don't need to know your heritage, or if you're white you don't need to know where you come from, or whatever. It's not on that vibe, it's the vibe of just saying you're human, and it's time to think in terms of humanity.

"Actually, any system of economics that doesn't practise higher ways of thinking, or should I say doesn't practise the more inner ways of thinking, is basically a doomed system. Capitalism definitely shows itself to be a doomed system because it does not concentrate on the person, it concentrates on what the person can do. This is detrimentally wrong. Yes, it produces alienation, but any system that doesn't work has the people running away from each other, trying to get away from it all. This system just does not work. It works right now, it's probably the best system we have, because of our lack of understanding of ourselves. If we had a better understanding of ourselves, this system would not need to exist. We can practise socialism, we might even be able to practise communism the way it is written down. Communism written down and socialism written down sound very good, until they're practised. When they're practised, people start to dislike them. Capitalism doesn't sound good when it's written down, yet people are satisfied with it as it's practised.

"If people really understood the system which they're working under, they wouldn't want to work under this system of capitalism, but they really don't know. I call this system the system of pimps and hoes [prostitutes]. One guy's a ho, one guy's a pimp, that's all it is. The ho works and works and works, and brings the money to the pimp. There's gotta be someone on the top, there's gotta be someone on the bottom. That's the capitalist system. But keep in mind it's the best system we've got if we don't know ourselves, and we don't know ourselves, which is why people walk around hating each other. Capitalism can

never ever ever work, because one man must be on the bottom and one man must be on the top for capitalism to work. But in the consciousness that we're in right this second, of me me me me me and my my my my my, this is the best system that we could possibly be under."

On censorship and identity...

"I'm for re-evolution. I would like to change the state which black people have evolved to. I would like to re-evolve. When you re-evolve something, that becomes a re-evolution. Revolution. This is why I call myself a black revolutionary, because I'd like to change the state which black people/humanity are in right now. Or should I say, I'd like to change the state in which humanity/black people are in right now.

"There's revolution going on right now. Just because I put out an album I've changed rap music – that's a revolution! The way people think of me is changing, that's revolution. This isn't the age of armed revolution yet. This is mental revolution. This battle is with education and history. Once we have a clear sense of who the real enemy is, then the armed revolution will definitely come out.

"They're trying to do everything they can to destroy music. Censorship is getting bad over here, but there again it's everything that America stands for. We have something called the First... *They* have something called the First Amendment, they give you the freedom of speech according to their laws, and nobody ever really studied the law anyway when it comes down to black people as a whole. We had no constitutional rights in this country, so it's no big deal now in 1990. People get all upset now because they think they're free, and when you tamper with people's freedom they get upset. But we're not free and I'm glad censorship is happening to wake people up to know they're not free. People can still tell you what not to say...

"Yeah, the blue-eyed black man. He's buggin', he's out of his mind. Any man or woman who tries to be something that they're not... I can understand make-up, I can even understand to some extent burning your hair, I can understand that for the sake of fashion or for the sake of fads. But when you start having surgery on your nose, and bleaching your skin to try and look lighter... White people go through the same shit, they go out and burn their skin to look darker. When you go to these extremes, to try and look like something you are absolutely not, that's when I have to question it. Are you really sane? Do you know what you're doing? Everybody does the same thing. The grass is greener on the other side. Black people want to be white, white people want to be black. That's the bottom line."

On the new wave of hardcore rappers...

"There are two sides to this coin. One side is that many of these artists don't know what they should be thinking. Most of them jump into the picture thinking that 'hardcore' is racism, in other words

they say 'If I come out and be pro-black dissin' all the white people, I'm hardcore'. That's one side. The other side is that the masses of the people have never been approached by a humanist. When you say you're a humanist people think of sandals, ripped up clothes all stringy – the 'hippy' look of the 60's. That's not what a humanist is – I am a humanist.

"The NWA situation is that they believe you have to come hardcore – they've never been approached by a humanist. Now that's why I think HEAL is so important because, here is KRS-One supposed to be pro-black, and everyone thinks I'm all about Africa, Africa, Africa; which I am, but I'm not pro-Africa, I'm pro-human because I can't say that the origination of the human race was in Africa without calling the Africans humanists. So my point with HEAL in terms of that is to challenge, I would like to challenge the pro-black philosophies of the X Clan or the Poor Righteous Teachers and others that are professing something conscious to an extent."

On the 'Sex And Violence' album...

As the title suggests, KRS-One's last album as BDP (in 1992) appeared to be a reversal of his recent humanist stance. But, as he explains, it served a specific purpose.

"'Sex And Violence' is really my first album. Everything you've heard previously to 'Sex And Violence' really doesn't exist in the marketplace. The kids that are listening and buying music right now, they don't know anything

★ **Knowledge Reigns Supreme Over Everyone – the 'edutainer' KRS-One drops some live science**

about 'By All Means Necessary' and they're probably just up on 'Edutainment' [his 1990 'message' album, mostly bypassed by punters and press, aggrieved at its musical shortcomings]. Now the kids before that, they've been into it, but now they got jobs, they got pressures, and they ain't got time to be hanging 'round the street. The kids out now don't know anything about Grandmaster Flash or Run DMC, know nothing of 'Criminal Minded' or Public Enemy's first album. To them, 'Sex And Violence' is my first album and sex and violence is the head of the Average Joe. They don't know nothing about these other albums. They wouldn't interest them."

"I realised that it's not enough to be conscious, or positive, or advocate a revolution in this industry. You have to compete if you want to stay out. This is my competition album, my 'bump all rappers' album. Now after this, I can continue, but I have to establish an audience, I have to rock them. When I came out with 'Criminal Minded' I had to establish to them that I was the ultimate rap artist that ever lived on the planet. Period! Now it's time to just break away for a minute and be about beats, lyrics and concepts. Just like I come out to establish what is edutainment and what is ghetto music, I've come out to establish what is rap. 'Sex And Violence' is rap. That is what rap music sounds like. This is the year I re-establish myself as the ultimate lyricist. The one who drops the beats that everyone else samples, the one that drops the lyrical styles.

"There's only one queen, that's Latifah. There's only one king, that's Run DMC. There's only one teacher, that's KRS-One. I think that everybody from NWA to Hammer is soft. I'm like Coca-Cola and other rappers are Diet-Coke. They want to do rap but they don't want to do hip-hop. Like Keith Haring [deceased artist who took graffiti into the art galleries], he was doing graffiti but he wasn't doing hip-hop culture. That's why Keith Haring will never get any respect from the street. Rest in peace Keith Haring, 'cos while you were alive we were dissing you and when you're dead it's no different. Rap is not something you should pay for. You should steal albums and sneak into concerts, that's rap.

"'Duck' is a message. You see messages don't always have to be positive. 'Duck' is a message to the gangster artist out there. There's been a lot of gangster activity and I remember when there was no gangsters out. I remember when Run DMC were the gangsters of rap. They were the hardcore gangster rappers and LL was the lover. He was just the mack. That's the era I come from. So the kids who grow up now and see NWA and think they're hard? That ain't hard. That's soft. That's pop actually.

"Black people don't really buy NWA. 'Straight Outta Compton' was dope, but 'Material Love' is hardcore. It hits the core, hard, Not 'I'll kill you' or 'I'm the baddest nigga on the block', that's not hardcore. When I said 'Tell me what the fuck am I supposed to do?' on 'Material

Love', all gangsters worldwide said, 'Yeah, what the fuck am I supposed to do? That's right! Yeah'. But at the end of the day they saw what time it was. When you fall in love with your gold chain and all that nonsense then this is what's going to happen. And they caught on and said 'Damn, that Kris, he got it going on'. That is hardcore."

On his following and his background...

"I stay true to the kids who buy my shit every year. You know when you see something that says BDP on it, it's not wack. Buy it, listen to it, chances are you're gonna get off. All I try to do is maintain that credibility with my audience. I don't care about no one else, I want to sell my 500,000, my little core who drive around in their jeeps every Friday and Saturday night, with their boom, boom sound.

"See, it's hard to explain the streets to the masses of people who aren't a part of the streets. You might know the streets, we might know, but to try and explain it to someone who grew up with a mother and father and ate every day... People say they're hungry when they're not, but to know what it's like to be really hungry is something I think that everybody should experience. I mean when I have a kid I'm gonna starve him. I'm gonna feed him and then starve him for a week. I'm not gonna buy him no food, He's gonna' starve, like when you're so hungry that you're throwing up bile, that green shit that be in your stomach. When you're hungry, you see food all around you, but

if you take any you go to jail. That shit is crazy! But if you've never lived it, it's hard to explain. The only thing I can say is, where I come from, homelessness, hunger and poverty is your friends, they stay with you forever. You never let go of poverty, hunger and homelessness. When you've been on the bottom...that's respect! That's where I come from. I don't come from the right and the wrong, I come from is. If I have to kill you, I will. If I have to kill myself to save you, I will. Where I come from, if you're in a hostage situation and you either kill your kids or kill yourself, who goes? I don't know if any one of you can answer that, but let me say my answer. The kids go. That's where I come from! I'm not saying that this way of thinking is right, I'd be the first to say I might be crazy, but this is where I'm at. This is me, here, in the street, in the coliseum, on the lecture tour, in the movie, on the video.

"This is the real deal. I don't advocate unnecessary violence but if you dis me I'm steppin' to you. That's how I'm living. If I get killed I'm killed. Fuck it! I'll have gone out like a champ."

On having a long rap career...

"I have a large older following, especially in America, because I've been out for seven years or so. These are the kids that grew up with me... Yes, we do have older fans, but they don't understand you, they never will, they never have. But they do understand intelligence, the need to move forward, the need to respect yourself and respect your people. My music stands for that, so they understand me. I can be as useful as I want to be, so long as I have the underlining self-respect and national respect.

"After we dropped 'Edutainment', we stated to taper off a little bit with putting out music. What happened was I started to have a conflict with Jive Records. When you have a problem with the record company, it always stagnates your career. Which is why I did all that stuff. It was kinda hype.

"See, me as an artist, I'm into music – consciousness-raising music. The bigger audiences these days, if it doesn't sell they don't want to hear it. And it's a Catch-22. Unless you're playing 'nigger, bitch, tramp, ho' you're not going to sell. I'm the one artist that has ultimate respect for all women in general, and African women in particular. I could never call any of our sisters a bitch, a tramp, nothing on that level. Even so much in my music today, even off the 'Criminal Minded' album, we used to make jokes at ourselves. Actually we called Scott [La Rock] a super ho! Because he was on the road buggin', so we called him that.

"Throughout my career from 'Ghetto Music' up to now there's just been this whole gangsta thing going on, while I was basically doing lectures. While everyone was running around yelling 'nigger, bitch, ho...', we were at universities discussing higher levels of thinking and talking about new ways to educate people, which really ain't a sellable item or isn't really

a musical item. But now on the street level in America, we are still the rulers and never left that.

"Some of these lectures allow the outside community to come in, some of them don't... But the black colleges here in America don't call me much. They're afraid of my message. My thing is about self-improvement. Black college don't want to hear that, they want to hear the white man is the devil, they want to hear 'kill whitey', 'pro-black, black, black'. That's not where I'm at.

"I've never really had a problem with white people at all. There's a few of course, every bunch, a few rejects. But that's with every race. That's a human thing. I received a lot of criticism for my humanist philosophy. I'm a human being before I'm black, before I'm African, before any of that I'm a human being, period. That's the philosophy I like to stick to, that's just the way I am. But to other artists that have a problem with the white man, they should just stay out of the stew. Stay out of his business thing

"I think rap now is very healthy as an art-form. But it's one of those things that's good while it's refrigerated. It's the difference between fresh squeezed and Tropicana juice. Tropicana's cool, it's good, it's orange juice. But fresh squeezed is the shit. That's the difference between rap and hip-hop. Hip-hop is fresh squeezed with seeds and pulp, you drink it and damn near choke. Rap is Tropicana. I and more people need that fresh squeezed...!

"BDP is large and what's happened is

I'm rebuilding and restructuring it. I had to fire the old members; they were leeches and parasites. The new members are more energetic. They don't see me as a threat, they see me more in themselves, are ready to do more for themselves, like Mad Lion, not just walk in my light. BDP these days are not really a music group, it's turned into more of a political organisation on the street level. Just glocks and knocks!

"In the future I hope to create BDP to be more of a political organisation, something like the Black Panther Party. But in the meantime we'll sing our way to victory. Mad Lion has launched the resurgence of BDP for the year 2000.

"I love a good gun record, personally. People debate about 'Oh, the violence'. To me, the only solution is revolution. As for women being called bitches, that's the majority of women and that's a bigger issue than music; that has to do with religion and education, the way people are brought up in life itself.

"On record I represent the consciousness of a certain type of audience so I say, 'Brown skin woman you a queen not a ho', and that's my responsibility. But I'm a minority in my message. The real message on the street is, 'I'm not a brown skin woman, I'm a black bitch'," he laughs at his own emphasis. "Yeah, don't care, I'm a hoooe!

"I think that I am the incarnation of God itself. Literally. I think that God is within me. When I walk the streets, if you ever wanted to see what God looks like – look at me. If someone else knew themselves to that point you could look at them too, it's not like I'm the only one.

"But I see me as God on Earth, and my job on this planet is to push the planet forward, make people know themselves, do the job of God. You know, followin' the creator of the universe is not reading, you can't read about God. Don't read about it, do it, act on it. And I say I'm not God, but I'm a manifestation, a flicker of sweat from the chin of the creator of the universe.

"So my little trivial job on this planet is rap, therefore there's no rapper that's gonna become better than me 'cos I, man, am d'king!" ■

public enemy

Perhaps the most famous and infamous group in the history of rap, Public Enemy were true innovators of the genre. The core membership of Chuck D, Hank Shocklee, Flavor Flav and DJ Terminator X first came together on Long Island in 1984. Other collaborators – including the notorious 'Minister of Information', Professor Griff – have come and gone, but the group's fusion of fast, furious beats and no-holds-barred rapping has stood the test of time remarkably well. Their début album, 'Yo! Bum Rush The Show', was released in 1987 to huge public and critical acclaim. But, unlike many contemporaries, PE just got better and better, with fine, no-compromise albums including 'Fear Of A Black Planet' and 'Apocalypse '91'.

★ public enemy

"There's a misunderstanding of what Afrocentricity is," says Chuck D, Public Enemy's fiercely authoritative rapper, explaining the concept behind the band's controversial third LP 'Fear Of A Black Planet' (1990). A former college radio DJ Chuck, alongside PE's famed production team The Bomb Squad, put together rap's most influential group in the early '80s while they were students at Adelphi University in Long Island. "Afrocentricity is a black basis. It deals with the majority of people on the planet, it's a sharing, loving thing. It's the same cultural basis as it was in Africa. It's not anything based on 'You might have your beliefs and I have my beliefs and we still get along together as equal human beings'. Also, it's not based on a complexion type thing. We get along together and I'm not judging you by your characteristics visually, I'm just judging by within. If you believe in the God I believe in, that there's a higher force and you have a respect for the planet and fellow human beings everything is cool. Afrocentricity is based around that whole thing.

"Eurocentricity is the exact opposite. It's somethin' that's beneficial to 10% of the world for the sake of white world supremacy. What it does, it disacknowledges the fact that white come from black, that the black man was the original man. There is no black and white. It's one or the other. It's black, and everybody sprouts from that. White's at the end of the line. It's not an opposite, 'cos there's not enough to be an opposite, it's only 10%. Black man can reproduce white easily, can produce somebody that's light skinned with blonde hair and blue eyes, y'know what I'm sayin'? All this is genetics, and scientists know this, but the common people don't, so they try to make somethin' up that doesn't exist at all.

"Throughout the years there's this belief that the white race is pure and people are stuck into that in a religious context and a racial context. They say 'If you're not down with this exclusive membership then you are fucked and if you can't get with it this way then fuck you'. Eurocentricity has been wicked to most of the people in the world, 90%, and my belief is that 100% of the planet should be shared by 100% of the people. Once it's acknowledged that everybody sprouts out of this original point you see all that other shit just go by the wayside.

"It's a challenge on the beliefs, traits and the religions or structure that's been built and set-up by supremists and racists for their benefit, in an exploitive way only benefiting aristocrats and governmental powers. There's a Professor at Howard University, Dr Frances Cress Welsing, and she says that if the world was truly to come together through the process of peace and love then this world accordin' to white world supremacy and racists would be somethin' other than white. Because you have the mixing in and the mingling, the mixing of cultures, the religions and all. That exclusive club would be diluted genetically. Racists look at that as being a dilution rather than just another complexion. You put black and white in a bowl it just turns into somethin' else, but they'll just call it 'non-white' which is black, and not part of the club. That's one of the reasons why we're seeing Eurocentricity and control, murder, lies, deceit, wars, imperialism, capitalism, takeovers, governmental exploitation... Everything's involved in Eurocentric points of view for the sake of white world supremacy. If you're not this then you're fucked.

"My whole point of view is that the priority and the initial concern is the uplifting of a black race and the rebuilding of the black male and the restructuring of the black man and

woman getting together to learn about themselves for self-defensive purposes. We have to learn about ourselves, number one as a safeguard and that's the number one I have to get across always.

"I deal with the struggle of black people and you gotta understand, even though people might consider myself and KRS-One as some sort of teacher, we're really despatchers of information. I only put an hour on an album, I only do as much as a two-hour show, so that's three hours a person can have contact with you. You can only do so much. So what we do is despatch our information, we point to the people that have been studying for 20, 30, 40 years.

"It's foolish to say that a rapper can come along and teach any of these sciences. What I consider myself a scientist in is some sort of media conquest or media control – opening the lines of communication through rap and words across to an audience that's willing to listen and get their curiosity sparked.

"People search for black culture and a perspective that's always been kept away from them. But white kids will have to face racism in another way, because racism was taught to the black people in America, even abroad, by a white system, and so distrust has developed. The distrust eliminates once you have an understanding of the situation, you become less naive and less defensive. And black people in general have to learn about themselves and be less naive and less defensive in that sense, but defensive against the system and how they're gonna work and network amongst each other. It's all about unity because the enemy is twice as intelligent and twice as strong.

"White kids have held onto it. It's a struggle for white kids to hold onto Afrocentricity. What's happenin' now in the States is that white kids are growin' up, and their system is a set of beliefs that's standard, and they go on up and say 'Well, I just wanna kick it'. For example, I'm producin' this 'white' group of rappers from Long Island [who were eventually christened, not without irony, Young Black Teenagers]. One of the kids has a daily struggle with his father because he's not like his other brothers. His father tells him plenty of times, 'Why are you comin' home with this nigger shit?' So that's a little bit of the struggle."

On the hip-hop genre...

"I'm the ultimate rap fan. I do a lot of rap studyin', and I study markets and when we go to different towns I talk to the people, I study the people a lot closer maybe than other rap artists do. I seen a lot of 'em come and go, and my whole thing is that your family, your audience, is your number one thing, but if you can't think like they think then you'll lose 'em. It's just a matter of acknowledging your audience and keep givin' them what they want without forfeiting your stuff. Some rappers are tryin' to please an American audience and just ignore the international audience, and you get caught up in tryin'

to appease the pop audience. I've always ignored the pop audience. Even though we're with Rush [managerial subsidiary of Def Jam and run by the label's co-founder, Russell Simmons]; they might say 'Well, this is advisable', I'll say 'Fuck that, I'm doin' what I do 'cos I know my audience'. I know the rap audience better than most performers. Rap's the only thing I buy and it's the only thing I'm into.

"The whole key is that everybody's come to it, white and black. There's people embedded in authority that ain't goin' for it, and they always fight, but that makes it fun. The music critics over in Britain that cover rap music, they're two beats late. And they're 'Oh, when Public Enemy or this hardcore shit dies what a relief it is', because they can get into something that's easier like De La Soul or A Tribe Called Quest, which is good music, but it's a section of the rap world. The Ice-Ts, the NWAs, they'll definitely be there."

On the music industry and big business...

"We have to be aware of corporate business more than ever. We need to keep an eye on the dollar. It has nothing to do with rhymes and tracks, it has to do with your particular business stance and your commitment to the consumer. If in these times there are going to be 20 white rappers coming out in 1996 because it's their – the record companies' – business, then what I'm saying is that we've got to make it our business too. We need to own 15, 18 of those white rappers. We've either gotta buy the record label or buy the group!

"Jackie Wilson is what I'm talking about. Elvis was a copy of Jackie Wilson, but can you imagine Jackie Wilson owning 25-30% of Elvis? A lot of rappers don't seem to be very broad with their rhymes. They're looking more for the tracks and the grooves and things like that, and one day they're going to find themselves crying because they had something stolen from them, whether it's their contract or whatever. In the music industry there's a simple rule: if you don't make your money, somebody else will. Right now there's too much emphasis being placed on the music and not enough placed on the business and when that happens guys like your Vanilla Ices come through. People can't even get mad about it 'cos you're gonna have no say as you were too worried about the rhymes at the time. You gotta think about the rhyme and the beats sure, but why make something some motherfucker is going to take? What amazes me me is that we have rappers out there that don't even respect rap history, so how are they going to talk about black or white history? I'm working with Grandmaster Flash right now on the Juice soundtrack [the rap-based film directed by Spike Lee's cinematographer Ernest Dickerson] and part of mine and Hank Shocklee's legacy is to always work with those that came before you, and always hold a place in the history of rap. You gotta support the music they made.

"Just doing shit for the thrill of it,

that's for fucking adolescents. Games is strictly for kids right? Well it's been a long time since I was a kid. I'm past kindergarten!"

Indeed, born Carlton Ridenhour in 1960, Chuck is now widely regarded as one of rap's eldest and most thoughtful statesmen.

"The point is that we gotta control what we create. It has nothing to do with black labels or white labels, but if you don't control the label or the distribution then you ain't shit. The United States is a vast country and the reason why the 25 million blacks aren't communicating like they do in Britain is because you gotta trek 3000 miles back and forth for anything to happen. You can't build something without constant communication..."

On community and religion...

"We ran our community before we became Public Enemy, so now we've got to get back there as the Public Enemy and try to build up youth centres, try to keep the churches from buying everything up and not even motivating the youth, and try to kick some of the corruption out of the political system – catch some of the people in government who are getting the money and not doing the job and get them kicked the fuck out of the place. We'll face a lot of shit – but then we always did.

"What you've got to understand is that when people get into religion, it's just a competitive thing. It doesn't mean that you're anti anything, it just means you favour one religious opinion over anther. I think the problem is with people confusing that with the scenario of people against people. What it boils down to is that Mr [Reverend Louis] Farrakhan is speaking from a Muslim point of view: he's not anti-Christian, anti-Semitic or anti-anything. He may favour the Koran as an interpretation of how we should live, but people shouldn't translate that into a dislike of people – it's just a disagreement of philosophy.

"Like, say you hear a Rabbi talking in a synagogue, then he's trying to say that other religions don't touch base quite as much as his – it's a religious conversation you know, and we should leave religious disagreements with the ministers. That's their battleground.

"There's only one true religion and that's that God gave light to the world for us to respect and share the planet – after that everything's just interpretation...

"Hitler was talking to a whole group of people who were looking for a scapegoat for their problems, but Mr Farrakhan's just looking to instill some sort of pride and self-sufficiency and some kind of leadership qualities in all of us. It's not like he always says that he's the one. He wants us to look at ourselves as individuals and realise that we're the ones and we must all do this together. In the US, the media take such philosophical religious talk as anti-humanist, but I think you have to disconnect religion and spiritual talk from social talk."

In 1987 Chuck became the first rapper to openly speak about and sample

Minister Louis Farrakhan, leader of the Nation of Islam and a man he describes as "a prophet".

Throughout the '80s and '90s the Minister's teachings have been shrouded in controversy with many whites and jews labelling them both racist and anti-Semitic – charges Farrakhan has consistently denied. Since then he has risen to a position where he can claim to represent many of the diverse voices in the black community. With Chuck and PE leading the way, hundreds of rappers have either drawn from the Nation's teachings, sampled speeches or offered praises to its leader. The extent of Farrakhan's popularity was exemplified by the impressive turn out for the Million Man March to Washington DC in October 1995.

"The Western Government has fallen victim to this church and state philosophy, to the extent where you find 'In God We Trust' written on a dollar bill. What's God got to do with a dollar bill? What's God got to do with Government? I mean fuck that man. What people choose as their personal religion should be totally separate from anything. The thing is that black people were trying to talk about the hell of the American system, and that's got nothing to do with religion, it's got something to do with black people trying to come out of a genocide that was set up for them by the Western world.

"Now this is why I say the planet must be shared. Africa was a place that could have been shared, but the European went

★ **Chuck D (left) & Flavor Flav bring the noise**

into Africa, took what he wanted, killed people off, took people to work in other places, kept the money and kept the goods for the sake of envy and greed and all the other things that come under devilish text... So black people are slaves, slaves from a slave state, and black Americans are living with the effect of this today. I still consider [Louis Farrakhan's] Nation of Islam to hold the best plan for every black man and woman to re-establish themselves as true equals rather than a   people being given equality."

On the evolution of PE...

"Our attitude to music is a cross between a sports team and military corps: win, crush, destroy. We're out there to get a point across, and we've got a strategy, you know what I'm saying? I just try to do what I can do to entertain – no limits, no restraints. In the States our tour with Anthrax [a thrash metal band who joined PE to re-record their early classic 'Bring Tha Noise' in 1991 – a pivotal rap/rock crossover record] was seen as very innovative; in Britain it became a kind of political story. But I think in the US people definitely recognised something new.

"The record company wanted a greatest hits compilation, but we felt we had no hits yet. There's no such thing as a PE hit...so we gave them 'Greatest Misses', just to be different.

"Our core audience admire us when we take stands, when we are weirdly different. I didn't pick the best records,

just the ones that were laying around and were off. I know I could make a star-studded album, but 1992 wasn't the time for it.

"God forbid, I could've died in a plane crash and what would've happened to the material in the vaults? They would've dug them out anyway!"

Nonetheless, what essentially amounted to a remix album was only warmly received, even if it was only intended as a stop gap release between tours.

"We came out to Roosevelt, Long Island to be fans of hip-hop again, check out the environment, hang with our kids. Work on some new material and try and build a solid foundation for the next five years. You can't do that touring every month.

"In the last two years one major goal was to shut down one era of Public Enemy and start another one. Also to get accustomed to the area that I grew up in, since we were on 26 tours in six years. Thirty-five countries, every single continent, all in the name of rap. I thought it was a time for me to get back to my roots and re-group. Just be a fan of rap, especially in the last year and a half. I had such a great time I almost don't want it to end. But it's time to be trend-setting again.

"People also always expect you to repeat what you've done in the past. People wanted another 'Yo! Bum Rush The Show', then we made 'It Takes A Nation..', then they wanted another 'Takes...'! Each album we make is different, love it or hate it. The reason people wanted us to repeat 'Takes A Nation' [released in '88, this tour-de-force is still widely regarded as the greatest rap album of all time] was because we sped up the hip-hop beats and no-one had done stuff that fast before. There'd never been any clutter. We do the unexpected. We mess with soundscapes, slowing groups down, ghostly noises. On 'Fear Of A Black Planet' we stripped things down. On 'Greatest Misses' they expected that and didn't get it.

"Now you all don't think we can rock shit. It's like Muhammed Ali, people didn't think he could come back.

"Age has a lot to do with it. At 33 and a third, I'm not thinking about the present. We're making offensive moves like basketball, it's for you all to figure out what we'll do next.

"In the first era of Public Enemy, we came into the rap situation with a certain set of goals. We achieved every goal we set out to do. The first thing that got me involved with rap was because I said I wanted to make a rap group that was as big as Run DMC. I wanted to change how people looked at rap music. I wanted to change how black people thought of ourselves. And we had the goal of building 5,000 political black leaders in America and across the world. Basically making each and every black person aware of who they were. That was a goal.

"I remember in 1985, people didn't know who Malcolm X was and they were damn well saying, '... to hell with Martin Luther King', so when we set out to be, we wanted to make a group that went out to every part of the planet in the name of rap. And I wanted to transcend rap and make rap just as big as any other musical form.

"In 1986, we felt there was a direction if we planned it properly; all of us could get into the music business through the name of rap, hence the title of the first release 'Yo! Bum Rush The Show'. When I finally took a deal, I said if it was something that just can't work for me, even though Rick [Rubin, Def Jam's other co-founder, who cajoled Chuck for nearly two years to sign a recording contract] wants me to rap, this is what's going to come out. We're going to push the doors of the industry. Harry [Allen – PE's publicist and self-styled 'Media Assassin'] went into journalism. Bill [Stepney] became an executive of the record company, Hank Shoklee went into producing, Dr Dre went into television. I went into Public Enemy."

"'Yo! Bum Rush The Show' meant bum rushing the gates of the industry, that looked upon rap as being a bastard music. In '86, we pushed the doors down, made some plans, made some goals and set out to achieve them. What I take offense to are people trying to guess how I thought. That what I did was clever marketing."

On growing up in the '60s...

"You have to remember I was born in 1960, so it was easy for me to put one and one together. My mother and father always dealt me the hardcore facts of

★ **Welcome to the terrordome – Chuck and Flav bum rush the show**

being black in America.

"I remember when Malcom X got shot and killed – I was five at the time. I was eight when Dr Martin Luther King got shot. I had to leave school early. I remember when The Panthers came about in 1969 and '70. I was part of the Lunch Program in Long Island NY. They had the lunch system hooked up in the African-American experience at Hofstra University. So I was a part of these things in the '60s.

"Rappers rap about what they know about and this was something I knew about. I wasn't 17, born in '69 rapping about the late '70s and disco or frivolous adolescent pursuits. I was rapping about things I grew up with, because I was ten years older than the average rappers. I loved rap and I loved black people, so it wasn't a marketing thing like people say. It wasn't. I was just rapping about what I knew, about something very few people could rap about because of my age, and being in the right time at the right place. That was the beginning of Public Enemy.

"I understood what was going on as a child because I had my people to tell me. My people were very informative, they told me who I was. I remember there was a tendency to call us 'negro' or 'coloured' and my Moms said 'No, you're black!', my Pa said 'You're black'.

"At eight, nine and ten, I was aware of what was going on. Even in the music, James Brown's 'Say It Loud, I'm Black And I'm Proud', I remember that was a turning point for people, who said 'We're not saying we're coloured no more. We're

black. You're black and you're proud!'. That was something that stuck. My Moms listening to Motown and soul, my uncles listening to Curtis Mayfield and Otis Redding, all kinds of music and my father listening to James Brown and jazz. All that stuff just seeped into me.

"Music is our environment, music is our culture and part of us, like the air is part of us. All the '60s music influenced not just me, but also the people that made PE's music. Hank, Eric, Keith. It's not something that's planned, it's not analytical, it's something that's naturally a part of us because we were older. We remember. Yeah, someone can go back and buy Smokey Robinson's 'Tears Of A Clown', but I remember when 'Tears Of A Clown' was out! Heh Heh!

"I don't mind showing my age because that's my advantage over everyone out there in the rap field, except Ice-T or whatever. And the fact I know and love rap so much and well, I'm an excellent student of it. You can't fault me that I'm a student in 11th grade and everyone else is in seventh grade. I'm just ahead because I'm older. Age should be looked upon as a blessing.

"You go to parts of Africa that Public Enemy set foot on in the winter of '92, all thanks to God, people there, the elders, they have the most props [respect]. In the States, because we're a plantation state, they teach you that when you're young you get the most props, you're old, you're disposable. In the rap game my advantage is my age. I ain't keeping no secrets. I don't front, I never said I was

21. I just never told people my age, but I never kept it a secret either. Age is a number, it's what keeps PE in the game..."

On musical influences...

"When I was growing up I listened to Sly & The Family Stone, James Brown, George Clinton, but I also listened to rock music. The music in Public Enemy is a reflection of what I listened to in the early '70s. Led Zeppelin and all the inroads made in rock. I grew up when there was a melting pot in music. After music became particled out – black music, white music – I think that stunted the music growth of people.

"When we make music, we reflect that historical melting pot. A lot of people view our music as being far to the left and crazy. But it's the fruit punch of music – a wild blend of all kinds of juices.

"I detest people who are lacking in musical knowledge. They say, 'Where does PE come off doing rockish music?'. My first record I did was 'Sophisticated Bitch', I did rock, I had Vernon 'Living Colour' Reid on it. Different aspects of our soundscape reflect our musical heritage. Rock 'n' roll is our music anyway. And rap music means rap over music – the original meaning of rap anyway. It was an overdub. When people say real hip-hop beats, they don't know what the fuck they're talking about. What does that mean? The original, early rap guys used rock records because a lot of black groups were doing disco type things. Besides, the real problem is controlling our own music and garnering the finances of it, not what we rap over."

On PE 'making it'...

"We got full acceptance when we hit Soul Train [hugely popular US black entertainment show] in 1988. Everything went from east to west, we were first accepted in Philly. We always respected the British audience from London to Birmingham. Blacks there are either from Caribbean or African roots, they were very receptive. It was actually harder to crack it here [in America] because people were still in the slave-like mentality. It still exists in England too, but they have their Caribbean roots and it's in the back of their minds. Somewhere our Afrocentrism was lost and it had to be connected there somewhere.

"It was fun while it was difficult to break. The movements of the '60s was still embedded in the older folks, but the kids (older teens) were open to it if we got to the people that were in charge of the message mediums, like the radio stations and other outlets, so that was the big barrier. We wanted to show the necessity of knowing one's self. To know about us.

"It caught on in 1988, we went to every city and issued a campaign – which was 'Bring Back Nationalism' at any cause, because it saved our ass. Also combining rap. One on one – the combination was lethal.

"It happened real fast. I got to build a group that's as big as Run DMC, the greatest rap group of all time, in terms of longevity, innovation and togetherness, humbleness, all that. We were actually discovered by them. We developed the art of rap touring to a science. Right where we could tour with U2 [in 1991], because we represented our art form. We were one of the best opening groups or middle groups. We soon became one of the best opening groups, but no-one wanted to play after us. We then became headliners. So we had to come up with different ways to stay on top."

On going back on the road...

"It was fun; it reminded us of when we started when no-one knew who we were. We had something to prove. We got a big response. We were like the underdogs. But we go by the PE rule, we go anywhere and prove we have the guts to say anything to anybody.

"Touring with Anthrax and U2 showed us what we didn't have when we were touring on a rap tour. When we tour now people say we run our tour like the government. We have nothing but good things to learn from touring with these guys. And we bring all these elements to rap. Crunch, my assistant, became the first rap lighting man. In the past you got guys on tour with you who took 40 gigs to get to know the correct lighting for your show.

"PE do different types of tours. You see different crowds depending on where it is and who's on the bill. We weren't mellowing, we just wanted to try something different. In 1991, we were on three different tours – we did an alternative tour, we did a heavy metal tour and a straight up hip-hop tour. The rap packers will only see you once, you can't come into the same city and expect people to see you twice without new material.

"I was never into making laid-back music. I always loved making over the edge music that crashes. That's just what I'm about. My personal tastes in music infiltrate PE. I like breakneck speeds and panic music. That type of music was easier for us to perform. Our music is hectic and the audience gets hectic.

"We always have energy on stage. That slower music is great, but it ain't got no energy on stage; you have to get blunted and you got to be laidback to appreciate it. The West Coast stuff, that funk and bluesy stuff, you got to understand the setting. You got to be driving along the road with your homie...

"We didn't play special music for the heavy metal audience either. We do the same shit, with a few tiny changes. Terminator's on the tables, me and Flavor are rapping. It's the same show, too. To those people who say we're mellow, okay so we don't put bodies on stage and chainsaw them in half, we just do what we do. Why do we do it? Because we can!"

Or can they? Since this interview was conducted PE have announced their retirement from live performance, to concentrate on other activities. However, they still continue to write and record under the Public Enemy banner. ∎